A DAUGHTER
OF EVE

HONORE DE BALZAC

Translated By Katharine Prescott Wormeley

1st WORLD
LIBRARY
Literary Society

A Daughter of Eve

Honore de Balzac

© 1st World Library, 2006
PO Box 2211
Fairfield, IA 52556
www.1stworldlibrary.com
First Edition

LCCN: 2006907706

Softcover ISBN: 1-4218-2427-2
Hardcover ISBN: 1-4218-2327-6
eBook ISBN: 1-4218-2527-9

Purchase *"A Daughter of Eve"*
as a traditional bound book at:
www.1stWorldLibrary.com/purchase.asp?ISBN=1-4218-2427-2

1st World Library is a literary, educational organization
dedicated to:

- Creating a free internet library of downloadable ebooks

- Hosting writing competitions and offering book
publishing scholarships.

Interested in more 1st World Library books?
contact: literacy@1stworldlibrary.com
Check us out at: www.1stworldlibrary.com

1st World Library Literary Society

Giving Back to the World

"If you want to work on the core problem, it's early school literacy."

- James Barksdale, former CEO of Netscape

"No skill is more crucial to the future of a child, or to a democratic and prosperous society, than literacy."

- Los Angeles Times

Literacy... means far more than learning how to read and write... The aim is to transmit... knowledge and promote social participation."

- UNESCO

"Literacy is not a luxury, it is a right and a responsibility. If our world is to meet the challenges of the twenty-first century we must harness the energy and creativity of all our citizens."

- President Bill Clinton

"Parents should be encouraged to read to their children, and teachers should be equipped with all available techniques for teaching literacy, so the varying needs and capacities of individual kids can be taken into account."

- Hugh Mackay

DEDICATION

To Madame la Comtesse Bolognini, nee Vimercati.

If you remember, madame, the pleasure your conversation gave to a traveller by recalling Paris to his memory in Milan, you will not be surprised to find him testifying his gratitude for many pleasant evenings passed beside you by laying one of his works at your feet, and begging you to protect it with your name, as in former days that name protected the tales of an ancient writer dear to the Milanese.

You have an Eugenie, already beautiful, whose intelligent smile gives promise that she has inherited from you the most precious gifts of womanhood, and who will certainly enjoy during her childhood and youth all those happinesses which a rigid mother denied to the Eugenie of these pages. Though Frenchmen are taxed with inconstancy, you will find me Italian in faithfulness and memory. While writing the name of "Eugenie," my thoughts have often led me back to that cool stuccoed salon and little garden in the Vicolo dei Cappucini, which echoed to the laughter of that dear child, to our sportive quarrels and our chatter. But you have left the Corso for the Tre Monasteri, and I know not how you are placed there; consequently, I am forced to think of you, not among the charming things with which no doubt you have surrounded yourself, but like one of those fine figures due to Raffaelle, Titian, Correggio, Allori, which seem abstractions, so distant are they from our daily lives.

If this book should wing its way across the Alps, it will prove to you the lively gratitude and respectful friendship of

Your devoted servant,
De Balzac.

CHAPTER I

THE TWO MARIES

In one of the finest houses of the rue Neuve-des-Mathurins, at half-past eleven at night, two young women were sitting before the fireplace of a boudoir hung with blue velvet of that tender shade, with shimmering reflections, which French industry has lately learned to fabricate. Over the doors and windows were draped soft folds of blue cashmere, the tint of the hangings, the work of one of those upholsterers who have just missed being artists. A silver lamp studded with turquoise, and suspended by chains of beautiful workmanship, hung from the centre of the ceiling. The same system of decoration was followed in the smallest details, and even to the ceiling of fluted blue silk, with long bands of white cashmere falling at equal distances on the hangings, where they were caught back by ropes of pearl. A warm Belgian carpet, thick as turf, of a gray ground with blue posies, covered the floor. The furniture, of carved ebony, after a fine model of the old school, gave substance and richness to the rather too decorative quality, as a painter might call it, of the rest of the room. On either side of a large window, two etageres displayed a hundred precious trifles, flowers of mechanical art brought into bloom by the fire of thought. On a chimney-piece of slate-blue marble were figures in old Dresden, shepherds in bridal garb, with delicate bouquets in their hands, German fantasticalities surrounding a platinum clock, inlaid with arabesques. Above it sparkled the brilliant facets of a Venice mirror framed in ebony, with figures carved in relief, evidently obtained from some former royal residence. Two jardinieres were filled with the exotic product of a hot-house, pale, but divine flowers, the treasures of botany.

In this cold, orderly boudoir, where all things were in place as if for sale, no sign existed of the gay and capricious disorder of a happy home. At the present moment, the two young women were weeping. Pain seemed to predominate. The name of the owner, Ferdinand du Tillet, one of the richest bankers in Paris, is enough to explain the luxury of the whole house, of which this boudoir is but a sample.

Though without either rank or station, having pushed himself forward, heaven knows how, du Tillet had married, in 1831, the daughter of the Comte de Granville, one of the greatest names in the French magistracy, - a man who became peer of France after the revolution of July. This marriage of ambition on du Tillet's part was brought about by his agreeing to sign an acknowledgment in the marriage contract of a dowry not received, equal to that of her elder sister, who was married to Comte Felix de Vandenesse. On the other hand, the Granvilles obtained the alliance with de Vandenesse by the largeness of the "dot." Thus the bank repaired the breach made in the pocket of the magistracy by rank. Could the Comte de Vandenesse have seen himself, three years later, the brother-in-law of a Sieur Ferdinand DU Tillet, so-called, he might not have married his wife; but what man of rank in 1828 foresaw the strange upheavals which the year 1830 was destined to produce in the political condition, the fortunes, and the customs of France? Had any one predicted to Comte Felix de Vandenesse that his head would lose the coronet of a peer, and that of his father-in-law acquire one, he would have thought his informant a lunatic.

Bending forward on one of those low chairs then called "chaffeuses," in the attitude of a listener, Madame du Tillet was pressing to her bosom with maternal tenderness, and occasionally kissing, the hand of her sister, Madame Felix de Vandenesse. Society added the baptismal name to the surname, in order to distinguish the countess from her sister-in-law, the Marquise Charles de Vandenesse, wife of the former ambassador, who had married the widow of the Comte de Kergarouet, Mademoiselle Emilie de Fontaine.

Half lying on a sofa, her handkerchief in the other hand, her breathing choked by repressed sobs, and with tearful eyes, the countess had been making confidences such as are made only from sister to sister when two sisters love each other; and these two sisters did love each other tenderly. We live in days when sisters married into such antagonist spheres can very well not love each other, and therefore the historian is bound to relate the reasons of this tender affection, preserved without spot or jar in spite of their husbands' contempt for each other and their own social disunion. A rapid glance at their childhood will explain the situation.

Brought up in a gloomy house in the Marais, by a woman of narrow mind, a "devote" who, being sustained by a sense of duty (sacred phrase!), had fulfilled her tasks as a mother religiously, Marie-Angelique and Marie Eugenie de Granville reached the period of their marriage - the first at eighteen, the second at twenty years of age - without ever leaving the domestic zone where the rigid maternal eye controlled them. Up to that time they had never been to a play; the churches of Paris were their theatre. Their education in their mother's house had been as rigorous as it would have been in a convent. From infancy they had slept in a room adjoining that of the Comtesse de Granville, the door of which stood always open. The time not occupied by the care of their persons, their religious duties and the studies considered necessary for well-bred young ladies, was spent in needlework done for the poor, or in walks like those an English-woman allows herself on Sunday, saying, apparently, "Not so fast, or we shall seem to be amusing ourselves."

Their education did not go beyond the limits imposed by confessors, who were chosen by their mother from the strictest and least tolerant of the Jansenist priests. Never were girls delivered over to their husbands more absolutely pure and virgin than they; their mother seemed to consider that point, essential as indeed it is, the accomplishment of all her duties toward earth and heaven. These two poor creatures had never, before their marriage, read a tale, or heard of a romance; their very drawings were of figures whose anatomy would have been masterpieces of the impossible to Cuvier, designed to feminize the Farnese Hercules himself. An old maid taught them drawing. A worthy priest instructed them in grammar, the French language, history, geography, and the very little arithmetic it was thought necessary in their rank for women to know. Their reading, selected from authorized books, such as the "Lettres Edifiantes," and Noel's "Lecons de Litterature," was done aloud in the evening; but always in presence of their mother's confessor, for even in those books there did sometimes occur passages which, without wise comments, might have roused their imagination. Fenelon's "Telemaque" was thought dangerous.

The Comtesse de Granville loved her daughters sufficiently to wish to make them angels after the pattern of Marie Alacoque, but the poor girls themselves would have preferred a less virtuous and more amiable mother. This education bore its natural fruits. Religion, imposed as a yoke and presented under its sternest aspect, wearied with formal practice these innocent young hearts, treated as sinful. It repressed their feelings, and was never precious to them, although it struck its roots deep down into their natures. Under such training the two Maries would either have become mere imbeciles, or they must necessarily have longed for independence. Thus it came to pass that they looked to marriage as soon as they saw anything of life and were able to compare a few ideas. Of their own tender graces and their personal value they were absolutely ignorant. They were ignorant, too, of their own innocence; how, then, could they know life? Without weapons to meet misfortune, without experience to appreciate happiness, they found no comfort in the maternal jail, all their joys were in each other. Their tender confidences at night in whispers, or a few short sentences exchanged if their mother left them for a moment, contained more ideas than the words themselves expressed. Often a glance, concealed from other eyes, by which they conveyed to each other their emotions, was like a poem of bitter melancholy. The sight of a cloudless sky, the fragrance of flowers, a turn in the garden, arm in arm, - these were their joys. The finishing of a piece of embroidery was to them a source of enjoyment.

Their mother's social circle, far from opening resources to their hearts or stimulating their minds, only darkened their ideas and depressed them; it was made up of rigid old women, withered and graceless, whose conversation turned on the differences which distinguished various preachers and confessors, on their own petty indispositions, on religious events insignificant even to the "Quotidienne" or "l'Ami de la Religion." As for the men who appeared in the Comtesse de Granville's salon, they extinguished any possible torch of love, so cold and sadly resigned were their faces. They were all of an age when mankind is sulky and fretful, and natural sensibilities are chiefly exercised at table and on the things relating to personal comfort. Religious egotism had long dried up those hearts devoted to narrow duties and entrenched behind pious practices. Silent games of cards occupied the whole evening, and the two young girls under the ban of that Sanhedrim enforced by maternal severity, came to hate the dispiriting personages about them with their hollow eyes and scowling faces.

On the gloom of this life one sole figure of a man, that of a music-master, stood vigorously forth. The confessors had decided that music was a Christian art, born of the Catholic Church and developed within her. The two Maries were therefore permitted to study music. A spinster in spectacles, who taught singing and the piano in a neighboring convent, wearied them with exercises; but when the eldest girl was ten years old, the Comte de Granville insisted on the importance of giving her a master. Madame de Granville gave all the value of conjugal obedience to this needed concession,

- it is part of a devote's character to make a merit of doing her duty.

The master was a Catholic German; one of those men born old, who seem all their lives fifty years of age, even at eighty. And yet, his brown, sunken, wrinkled face still kept something infantile and artless in its dark creases. The blue of innocence was in his eyes, and a gay smile of springtide abode upon his lips. His iron-gray hair, falling naturally like that of the Christ in art, added to his ecstatic air a certain solemnity which was absolutely deceptive as to his real nature; for he was capable of committing any silliness with the most exemplary gravity. His clothes were a necessary envelope, to which he paid not the slightest attention, for his eyes looked too high among the clouds to concern themselves with such materialities. This great unknown artist belonged to the kindly class of the self-forgetting, who give their time and their soul to others, just as they leave their gloves on every table and their umbrella at all doors. His hands were of the kind that are dirty as soon as washed. In short, his old body, badly poised on its knotted old legs, proving to what degree a man can make it the mere accessory of his soul, belonged to those strange creations which have been properly depicted only by a German, - by Hoffman, the poet of that which seems not to exist but yet has life.

Such was Schmucke, formerly chapel-master to the Margrave of Anspach; a musical genius, who was now examined by a council of devotes, and asked if he kept the fasts. The master was much inclined to answer, "Look at me!" but how could he venture to joke with pious dowagers and Jansenist confessors? This apocryphal old fellow held such a place in the lives of the two Maries, they felt such friendship for the grand and simple-minded artist, who was happy and contented in the mere comprehension of his art, that after their marriage, they each gave him an annuity of three hundred francs a year, - a sum which sufficed to pay for his lodging, beer, pipes, and clothes. Six hundred francs a year and his lessons put him in Eden. Schmucke had never found courage to confide his poverty and his aspirations to any but these two adorable young girls, whose hearts were blooming beneath the snow of maternal rigor and the ice of devotion. This fact explains Schmucke and the girlhood of the two Maries.

No one knew then, or later, what abbe or pious spinster had discovered the old German then vaguely wandering about Paris, but as soon as mothers of families learned that the Comtesse de Granville had found a music-master for her daughters, they all inquired for his name and address. Before long, Schmucke had thirty pupils in the Marais. This tardy success was manifested by steel buckles to his shoes, which were lined with horse-hair soles, and by a more frequent change of linen. His artless gaiety, long suppressed by noble and decent poverty, reappeared. He gave vent to witty little remarks and flowery speeches in his German-Gallic patois, very observing and very quaint and said with an air which disarmed ridicule. But he was so pleased to bring a laugh to the lips of his two pupils, whose dismal life his sympathy had penetrated, that hc would gladly have made himself wilfully ridiculous had he failed in being so by nature.

According to one of the nobler ideas of religious education, the young girls always accompanied their master respectfully to the door. There they would make him a few kind speeches, glad to do anything to give him pleasure. Poor things! all they could do was to show him their womanhood. Until their marriage, music was to them another life within their lives, just as, they say, a Russian peasant takes his dreams for reality and his actual life for a troubled sleep. With the instinct of protecting their souls against the pettiness that threatened to overwhelm them, against the all-pervading asceticism of their home, they flung themselves into the difficulties of the musical art, and spent themselves upon it. Melody, harmony, and composition, three daughters of heaven, whose choir was led by an old Catholic faun drunk with music, were to these poor girls the compensation of their trials; they made them, as it were, a rampart against their daily lives. Mozart, Beethoven, Gluck, Paesiello, Cimarosa, Haydn, and certain secondary geniuses, developed in their souls a passionate emotion which never passed beyond the chaste enclosure of their breasts, though it permeated that other creation through which, in spirit, they winged their flight. When they had executed some great work in a manner that their master declared was almost faultless, they embraced each other in ecstasy and the old man called them his Saint Cecilias.

The two Maries were not taken to a ball until they were sixteen years of age, and then only four times a year in special houses. They were not allowed to leave their mother's side without instructions as to their behavior with their partners; and so severe were those instructions that they dared say only yes or no during a dance. The eye of the countess never left them, and she seemed to know from the mere movement of their lips the words they uttered. Even the ball-dresses of these poor little things were piously irreproachable; their muslin gowns came up to their chins with an endless number of thick ruches, and the sleeves came down to their wrists. Swathing in this way their natural charms, this costume gave them a vague resemblance to Egyptian hermae; though from these blocks of muslin rose enchanting little heads of tender melancholy. They felt themselves the objects of pity, and inwardly resented it. What woman, however innocent, does not desire to excite envy?

No dangerous idea, unhealthy or even equivocal, soiled the pure pulp of their brain; their hearts were innocent, their hands were horribly red, and they glowed with health. Eve did not issue more innocent from the hands of God than these two girls from their mother's home when they went to the mayor's office and the church to be married, after receiving the simple but terrible injunction to obey in all things two men with whom they were henceforth to live and sleep by day and by night. To their minds, nothing could be worse in the strange houses where they were to go than the maternal convent.

Why did the father of these poor girls, the Comte de Granville, a wise and upright magistrate (though sometimes led away by politics), refrain from protecting the helpless little creatures from such crushing despotism? Alas! by mutual understanding, about ten years after marriage, he and his wife were separated while living under one roof. The father had taken upon himself the education of his sons, leaving that of the daughters to his wife. He saw less danger for women than for men in the application of his wife's oppressive system. The two Maries, destined as women to endure tyranny, either of love or marriage, would be, he

Honore de Balzac

thought, less injured than boys, whose minds ought to have freer play, and whose manly qualities would deteriorate under the powerful compression of religious ideas pushed to their utmost consequences. Of four victims the count saved two.

The countess regarded her sons as too ill-trained to admit of the slightest intimacy with their sisters. All communication between the poor children was therefore strictly watched. When the boys came home from school, the count was careful not to keep them in the house. The boys always breakfasted with their mother and sisters, but after that the count took them off to museums, theatres, restaurants, or, during the summer season, into the country. Except on the solemn days of some family festival, such as the countess's birthday or New Year's day, or the day of the distribution of prizes, when the boys remained in their father's house and slept there, the sisters saw so little of their brothers that there was absolutely no tie between them. On those days the countess never left them for an instant alone together. Calls of "Where is Angelique?" - "What is Eugenie about?" - "Where are my daughters?" resounded all day. As for the mother's sentiments towards her sons, the countess raised to heaven her cold and macerated eyes, as if to ask pardon of God for not having snatched them from iniquity.

Her exclamations, and also her reticences on the subject of her sons, were equal to the most lamenting verses in Jeremiah, and completely deceived the sisters, who supposed their sinful brothers to be doomed to perdition.

When the boys were eighteen years of age, the count

gave them rooms in his own part of the house, and sent them to study law under the supervision of a solicitor, his former secretary. The two Maries knew nothing therefore of fraternity, except by theory. At the time of the marriage of the sisters, both brothers were practising in provincial courts, and both were detained by important cases. Domestic life in many families which might be expected to be intimate, united, and homogeneous, is really spent in this way. Brothers are sent to a distance, busy with their own careers, their own advancement, occupied, perhaps, about the good of the country; the sisters are engrossed in a round of other interests. All the members of such a family live disunited, forgetting one another, bound together only by some feeble tie of memory, until, perhaps, a sentiment of pride or self-interest either joins them or separates them in heart as they already are in fact. Modern laws, by multiplying the family by the family, has created a great evil, - namely, individualism.

In the depths of this solitude where their girlhood was spent, Angelique and Eugenie seldom saw their father, and when he did enter the grand apartment of his wife on the first floor, he brought with him a saddened face. In his own home he always wore the grave and solemn look of a magistrate on the bench. When the little girls had passed the age of dolls and toys, when they began, about twelve, to use their minds (an epoch at which they ceased to laugh at Schmucke) they divined the secret of the cares that lined their father's forehead, and they recognized beneath that mask of sternness the relics of a kind heart and a fine character. They vaguely perceived how he had yielded to the forces of religion in his household, disappointed as he was in his hopes of a husband, and wounded in the tenderest fibres of paternity, - the love of a father for his daughters. Such griefs were singularly moving to the hearts of the two young girls, who were themselves deprived of all tenderness. Sometimes, when pacing the garden between his daughters, with an arm round each little waist, and stepping with their own short steps, the father would stop short behind a clump of trees, out of sight of the house, and kiss them on their foreheads; his eyes, his lips, his whole countenance expressing the deepest commiseration.

"You are not very happy, my dear little girls," he said one day; "but I shall marry you early. It will comfort me to have you leave home."

"Papa," said Eugenie, "we have decided to take the first man who offers."

"Ah!" he cried, "that is the bitter fruit of such a system. They want to make saints, and they make -" he stopped without ending his sentence.

Often the two girls felt an infinite tenderness in their father's "Adieu," or in his eyes, when, by chance, he dined at home. They pitied that father so seldom seen, and love follows often upon pity.

This stern and rigid education was the cause of the marriages of the two sisters welded together by misfortune, as Rita-Christina by the hand of Nature. Many men, driven to marriage, prefer a girl taken from a convent, and saturated with piety, to a girl brought up to worldly ideas. There seems to be no middle course. A man must marry either an educated girl, who reads the newspapers and comments upon them, who waltzes with a dozen young men, goes to the theatre, devours novels, cares nothing for religion, and makes her own ethics, or an ignorant and innocent young girl, like either of the two Maries. Perhaps there may be as much danger with the one kind as with the other. Yet the vast majority of men who are not so old as Arnolphe, prefer a religious Agnes to a budding Celimene.

The two Maries, who were small and slender, had the same figure, the same foot, the same hand. Eugenie, the younger, was fair-haired, like her mother, Angelique was dark-haired, like the father. But they both had the same complexion, - a skin of the pearly whiteness which shows the richness and purity of the blood, where the color rises through a tissue like that of the jasmine, soft, smooth, and tender to the touch. Eugenie's blue eyes and the brown eyes of Angelique had an expression of artless indiffer-ence, of ingenuous surprise, which was rendered by the vague manner with which the pupils floated on the fluid whiteness of the eyeball. They were both well-made; the rather thin shoulders would develop later. Their throats, long veiled, delighted the eye when their husbands requested them to wear low dresses to a ball, on which occasion they both felt a pleasing shame, which made them first blush behind closed doors, and afterwards, through a whole evening in company.

On the occasion when this scene opens, and the eldest, Angelique, was weeping, while the younger, Eugenie, was consoling her, their hands and arms were white as milk. Each had nursed a child, - one a boy, the other a daughter. Eugenie, as a girl, was thought very giddy by her mother, who had therefore treated her with especial watchfulness and severity. In the eyes of that much-feared mother, Angelique, noble and proud, appeared to have a soul so lofty that it would guard itself, whereas, the more lively Eugenie needed restraint. There are many charming beings misused by fate, - beings who ought by rights to prosper in this life, but who live and die unhappy, tortured by some evil genius, the victims of unfortunate circumstances. The innocent and naturally light-hearted Eugenie had fallen into the hands and beneath the malicious despotism of a self-made man on leaving the maternal prison. Angelique, whose nature inclined her to deeper sentiments, was thrown into the upper spheres of Parisian social life, with the bridle lying loose upon her neck.

CHAPTER II

A CONFIDENCE BETWEEN SISTERS

Madame de Vandenesse, Marie-Angelique, who seemed to have broken down under a weight of troubles too heavy for her soul to bear, was lying back on the sofa with bent limbs, and her head tossing restlessly. She had rushed to her sister's house after a brief appearance at the Opera. Flowers were still in her hair, but others were scattered upon the carpet, together with her gloves, her silk pelisse, and muff and hood. Tears were mingling with the pearls on her bosom; her swollen eyes appeared to make strange confidences. In the midst of so much luxury her distress was horrible, and she seemed unable to summon courage to speak.

"Poor darling!" said Madame du Tillet; "what a mistaken idea you have of my marriage if you think that I can help you!"

Hearing this revelation, dragged from her sister's heart by the violence of the storm she herself had raised there, the countess looked with stupefied eyes at the banker's wife; her tears stopped, and her eyes grew fixed.

"Are you in misery as well, my dearest?" she said, in a

Honore de Balzac

low voice.

"My griefs will not ease yours."

"But tell them to me, darling; I am not yet too selfish to listen. Are we to suffer together once more, as we did in girlhood?"

"But alas! we suffer apart," said the banker's wife. "You and I live in two worlds at enmity with each other. I go to the Tuileries when you are not there. Our husbands belong to opposite parties. I am the wife of an ambitious banker, - a bad man, my darling; while you have a noble, kind, and generous husband."

"Oh! don't reproach me!" cried the countess. "To understand my position, a woman must have borne the weariness of a vapid and barren life, and have entered suddenly into a paradise of light and love; she must know the happiness of feeling her whole life in that of another; of espousing, as it were, the infinite emotions of a poet's soul; of living a double existence, - going, coming with him in his courses through space, through the world of ambition; suffering with his griefs, rising on the wings of his high pleasures, developing her faculties on some vast stage; and all this while living calm, serene, and cold before an observing world. Ah! dearest, what happiness in having at all hours an enormous interest, which multiplies the fibres of the heart and varies them indefinitely! to feel no longer cold indifference! to find one's very life depending on a thousand trifles! - on a walk where an eye will beam to us from a crowd, on a glance which pales the sun! Ah! what intoxication, dear, to live! to *live* when other women are praying on their knees for emotions that never come to them! Remember, darling, that for this poem of delight there is but a single moment, - youth! In a few years winter comes, and cold. Ah! if you possessed these living riches of the heart, and were threatened with the loss of them -"

Madame du Tillet, terrified, had covered her face with her hands during the passionate utterance of this anthem.

"I did not even think of reproaching you, my beloved," she said at last, seeing her sister's face bathed in hot tears. "You have cast into my soul, in one moment, more brands than I have tears to quench. Yes, the life I live would justify to my heart a love like that you picture. Let me believe that if we could have seen each other oftener, we should not now be where we are. If you had seen my sufferings, you must have valued your own happiness the more, and you might have strengthened me to resist my tyrant, and so have won a sort of peace. Your misery is an incident which chance may change, but mine is daily and perpetual. To my husband I am a peg on which to hang his luxury, the sign-post of his ambition, a satisfaction to his vanity. He has no real affection for me, and no confidence. Ferdinand is hard and polished as that piece of marble," she continued, striking the chimney-piece. "He distrusts me. Whatever I may want for myself is refused before I ask it; but as for what flatters his vanity and proclaims his wealth, I have no occasion to express a wish. He decorates my apartments; he spends enormous sums upon my entertainments; my servants, my opera-box, all external matters are maintained with the utmost splendor. His vanity spares no expense; he would trim his children's swaddling-clothes with lace if he could, but he would never hear their cries, or guess their needs. Do you understand me? I am covered with diamonds when I go to court; I wear the richest jewels in society, but I have not one farthing I can use. Madame du Tillet, who, they say, is envied, who appears to float in gold, has not a hundred francs she can call her own. If the father cares little for his child, he cares less for its mother. Ah! he has cruelly made me feel that he bought me, and that in marrying me without a 'dot' he was wronged. I might perhaps have won him to love me, but there's an outside influence against it, - that of a woman, who is over fifty years of age, the widow of a notary, who rules him. I shall never be free, I know that, so long as he lives. My life is regulated like that of a queen; my meals are served with the utmost formality; at a given hour I must drive to the Bois; I am always accompanied by two footmen in full dress; I am obliged to return at a certain hour. Instead of giving orders, I receive them. At a ball, at the theatre, a servant comes to me and says: 'Madame's carriage is ready,' and I am obliged to go, in the midst, perhaps, of something I enjoy. Ferdinand would be furious if I did not obey the etiquette he prescribes for his wife; he frightens me. In the midst of this hateful opulence, I find myself regretting the past, and thinking that our mother was kind; she left us the nights when we could talk together; at any rate, I was living with a dear being who loved me and suffered with me; whereas here, in this sumptuous house, I live in a desert."

At this terrible confession the countess caught her sister's hand and kissed it, weeping.

"How, then, can I help you," said Eugenie, in a low voice. "He would be suspicious at once if he surprised us here, and would insist on knowing all that you have been saying to me. I should be forced to tell a lie, which is difficult indeed with so sly and treacherous a man; he would lay traps for me. But enough of my own miseries; let us think of yours. The forty thousand francs you want would be, of course, a mere nothing to Ferdinand, who handles millions with that fat banker, Baron de Nucingen. Sometimes, at dinner, in my presence, they say things to each other which make me shudder. Du Tillet knows my discretion, and they often talk freely before me, being sure of my silence. Well, robbery and murder on the high-road seem to me merciful compared to some of their financial schemes. Nucingen and he no more mind destroying a man than if he were an animal. Often I am told to receive poor dupes whose fate I have heard them talk of the night before, - men who rush into some business where they are certain to lose their all. I am tempted, like Leonardo in the brigand's cave, to cry out, 'Beware!' But if I did, what would become of me? So I keep silence. This splendid house is a cut-throat's den! But Ferdinand and Nucingen will lavish millions for their own caprices. Ferdinand is now buying from the other du Tillet family the site of their old castle; he intends to rebuild it and add a forest with large domains to the estate, and make his son a count; he declares that by the third generation the family will be noble. Nucingen, who is tired of his house in the rue Saint-Lazare, is building a palace. His wife is a friend of mine - Ah!" she cried, interrupting herself, "she might help us; she is very bold with her husband; her fortune is in her own right. Yes, she could save you."

"Dear heart, I have but a few hours left; let us go to her this evening, now, instantly," said Madame de Vandenesse, throwing herself into Madame du Tillet's arms with a burst of tears.

"I can't go out at eleven o'clock at night," replied her sister.

"My carriage is here."

"What are you two plotting together?" said du Tillet, pushing open the door of the boudoir.

He came in showing a torpid face lighted now by a speciously amiable expression. The carpets had dulled his steps and the preoccupation of the two sisters had kept them from noticing the noise of his carriage-wheels on entering the court-yard. The countess, in whom the habits of social life and the freedom in which her husband had left her had developed both wit and shrewdness, - qualities repressed in her sister by marital despotism, which simply continued that of their mother, - saw that Eugenie's terror was on the point of betraying them, and she evaded that danger by a frank answer.

"I thought my sister richer than she is," she replied, looking straight at her brother-in-law. "Women are sometimes embarrassed for money, and do not wish to tell their husbands, like Josephine with Napoleon. I came here to ask Eugenie to do me a service."

"She can easily do that, madame. Eugenie is very rich," replied du Tillet, with concealed sarcasm.

"Is she?" replied the countess, smiling bitterly.

"How much do you want?" asked du Tillet, who was not sorry to get his sister-in-law into his meshes.

"Ah, monsieur! but I have told you already we do not

wish to let our husbands into this affair," said Madame de Vandenesse, cautiously, - aware that if she took his money, she would put herself at the mercy of the man whose portrait Eugenie had fortunately drawn for her not ten minutes earlier. "I will come to-morrow and talk with Eugenie."

"To-morrow?" said the banker. "No; Madame du Tillet dines to-morrow with a future peer of France, the Baron de Nucingen, who is to leave me his place in the Chamber of Deputies."

"Then permit her to join me in my box at the Opera," said the countess, without even glancing at her sister, so much did she fear that Eugenie's candor would betray them.

"She has her own box, madame," said du Tillet, nettled.

"Very good; then I will go to hers," replied the countess.

"It will be the first time you have done us that honor," said du Tillet.

The countess felt the sting of that reproach, and began to laugh.

"Well, never mind; you shall not be made to pay anything this time. Adieu, my darling."

"She is an insolent woman," said du Tillet, picking up the flowers that had fallen on the carpet. "You ought," he said to his wife, "to study Madame de Vandenesse. I'd like to see you before the world as insolent and overbearing as your sister has just been here. You have a silly, bourgeois air which I detest."

Eugenie raised her eyes to heaven as her only answer.

"Ah ca, madame! what have you both been talking of?" said the banker, after a pause, pointing to the flowers. "What has happened to make your sister so anxious all of a sudden to go to your opera-box?"

The poor helot endeavored to escape questioning on the score of sleepiness, and turned to go into her dressing-room to prepare for the night; but du Tillet took her by the arm and brought her back under the full light of the wax-candles which were burning in two silver-gilt sconces between fragrant nosegays. He plunged his light eyes into hers and said, coldly: -

"Your sister came here to borrow forty thousand francs for a man in whom she takes an interest, who'll be locked up within three days in a debtor's prison."

The poor woman was seized with a nervous trembling, which she endeavored to repress.

"You alarm me," she said. "But my sister is far too well brought up, and she loves her husband too much to be interested in any man to that extent."

"Quite the contrary," he said, dryly. "Girls brought up as you two were, in the constraints and practice of piety, have a thirst for liberty; they desire happiness, and the happiness they get in marriage is never as fine as that they dreamt of. Such girls make bad wives."

"Speak for me," said poor Eugenie, in a tone of bitter

feeling, "but respect my sister. The Comtesse de Vandenesse is happy; her husband gives her too much freedom not to make her truly attached to him. Besides, if your supposition were true, she would never have told me of such a matter."

"It is true," he said, "and I forbid you to have anything to do with the affair. My interests demand that the man shall go to prison. Remember my orders."

Madame du Tillet left the room.

"She will disobey me, of course, and I shall find out all the facts by watching her," thought du Tillet, when alone in the boudoir. "These poor fools always think they can do battle against us."

He shrugged his shoulders and rejoined his wife, or to speak the truth, his slave.

The confidence made to Madame du Tillet by Madame Felix de Vandenesse is connected with so many points of the latter's history for the last six years, that it would be unintelligible without a succinct account of the principal events of her life.

CHAPTER III

THE HISTORY OF A FORTUNATE WOMAN

Among the remarkable men who owed their destiny to the Restoration, but whom, unfortunately, the restored monarchy kept, with Martignac, aloof from the concerns of government, was Felix de Vandenesse, removed, with several others, to the Chamber of peers during the last days of Charles X. This misfortune, though, as he supposed, temporary, made him think of marriage, towards which he was also led, as so many men are, by a sort of disgust for the emotions of gallantry, those fairy flowers of the soul. There comes a vital moment to most of us when social life appears in all its soberness.

Felix de Vandenesse had been in turn happy and unhappy, oftener unhappy than happy, like men who, at their start in life, have met with Love in its most perfect form. Such privileged beings can never subsequently be satisfied; but, after fully experiencing life, and comparing characters, they attain to a certain contentment, taking refuge in a spirit of general indulgence. No one deceives them, for they delude themselves no longer; but their resignation, their disillusionment is always graceful; they expect what comes, and therefor they suffer less. Felix might still rank among the handsomest and most agreeable men in

Paris. He was originally commended to many women by one of the noblest creatures of our epoch, Madame de Mortsauf, who had died, it was said, out of love and grief for him; but he was specially trained for social life by the handsome and well-known Lady Dudley.

In the eyes of many Parisian women, Felix, a sort of hero of romance, owed much of his success to the evil that was said of him. Madame de Manerville had closed the list of his amorous adventures; and perhaps her dismissal had something to do with his frame of mind. At any rate, without being in any way a Don Juan, he had gathered in the world of love as many disenchantments as he had met with in the world of politics. That ideal of womanhood and of passion, the type of which - perhaps to his sorrow - had lighted and governed his dawn of life, he despaired of ever finding again.

At thirty years of age, Comte Felix determined to put an end to the burden of his various felicities by marriage. On that point his ideas were extremely fixed; he wanted a young girl brought up in the strictest tenets of Catholicism. It was enough for him to know how the Comtesse de Granville had trained her daughters to make him, after he had once resolved on marriage, request the hand of the eldest. He himself had suffered under the despotism of a mother; he still remembered his unhappy childhood too well not to recognize, beneath the reserves of feminine shyness, the state to which such a yoke must have brought the heart of a young girl, whether that heart was soured, embittered, or rebellious, or whether it was still peaceful, lovable, and ready to unclose to noble sentiments. Tyranny produces two opposite effects, the symbols of which exist in two grand figures of ancient slavery, Epictetus and Spartacus, - hatred and evil feelings on the one hand, resignation and tenderness, on the other.

The Comte de Vandenesse recognized himself in Marie-Angelique de Granville. In choosing for his wife an artless, innocent, and pure young girl, this young old man determined to mingle a paternal feeling with the conjugal feeling. He knew his own heart was withered by the world and by politics, and he felt that he was giving in exchange for a dawning life the remains of a worn-out existence. Beside those springtide flowers he was putting the ice of winter; hoary experience with young and innocent ignorance. After soberly judging the position, he took up his conjugal career with ample precaution; indulgence and perfect confidence were the two anchors to which he moored it. Mothers of families ought to seek such men for their daughters. A good mind protects like a divinity; disenchantment is as keen-sighted as a surgeon; experience as foreseeing as a mother. Those three qualities are the cardinal virtues of a safe marriage. All that his past career had taught to Felix de Vandenesse, the observations of a life that was busy, literary, and thoughtful by turns, all his forces, in fact, were now employed in making his wife happy; to that end he applied his mind.

When Marie-Angelique left the maternal purgatory, she rose at once into the conjugal paradise prepared for her by Felix, rue du Rocher, in a house where all things were redolent of aristocracy, but where the varnish of society did not impede the ease and "laisser-aller" which young and loving hearts desire so much. From the start, Marie-Angelique tasted all the sweets of material life to the very utmost. For two years her husband made himself, as it were, her purveyor. He explained to her, by degrees, and with great art, the things of life; he initiated her slowly into the mysteries of the highest society; he taught her the genealogies of noble families; he showed her the world; he guided her taste in dress; he trained her to converse; he took her from theatre to theatre, and made her study literature and current history. This education he accomplished with all the care of a lover, father, master, and husband; but he did it soberly and discreetly; he managed both enjoyments and instructions in such a manner as not to destroy the value of her religious ideas. In short, he carried out his enterprise with the wisdom of a great master. At the end of four years, he had the happiness of having formed in the Comtesse de Vandenesse one of the most lovable and remarkable young women of our day.

Marie-Angelique felt for Felix precisely the feelings with which Felix desired to inspire her, - true friendship, sincere gratitude, and a fraternal love, in which was mingled, at certain times, a noble and dignified tender-ness, such as tenderness between husband and wife ought to be. She was a mother, and a good mother. Felix had therefore attached himself to his young wife by every bond without any appearance of garroting her, - relying for his happiness on the charms of habit.

None but men trained in the school of life - men who have gone round the circle of disillusionment, political and amorous - are capable of following out a course like this. Felix, however, found in his work the same pleasure that painters, writers, architects take in their creations. He doubly enjoyed both the work and its fruition as he admired his wife, so artless, yet so well-informed, witty, but natural, lovable and chaste, a girl, and yet a mother, perfectly free, though bound by the chains of righteousness. The history of all good homes is that of prosperous peoples; it can be written in two lines, and has in it nothing for literature. So, as happiness is only explicable to and by itself, these four years furnish nothing to relate which was not as tender as the soft outlines of eternal cherubs, as insipid, alas! as manna, and about as amusing as the tale of "Astrea."

In 1833, this edifice of happiness, so carefully erected by Felix de Vandenesse, began to crumble, weakened at its base without his knowledge. The heart of a woman of twenty-five is no longer that of a girl of eighteen, any more than the heart of a woman of forty is that of a woman of thirty. There are four ages in the life of woman; each age creates a new woman. Vandenesse knew, no doubt, the law of these transformations (created by our modern manners and morals), but he forgot them in his own case, - just as the best grammarian will forget a rule of grammar in writing a book, or the greatest general in the field under fire, surprised by some unlooked-for change of base, forgets his military tactics. The man who can perpetually bring his thought to bear upon his facts is a man of genius; but the man of the highest genius does not display genius at all times; if he did, he would be like to God.

After four years of this life, with never a shock to the soul, nor a word that produced the slightest discord in this sweet concert of sentiment, the countess, feeling herself developed like a beautiful plant in a fertile soil, caressed by the sun of a cloudless sky, awoke to a sense of a new self. This crisis of her life, the subject of this Scene, would be incomprehensible without certain explanations, which may extenuate in the eyes of women the wrong-doing of this young countess, a happy wife, a happy mother, who seems, at first sight, inexcusable.

Life results from the action of two opposing principles; when one of them is lacking the being suffers. Vandenesse, by satisfying every need, had suppressed desire, that king of creation, which fills an enormous place in the moral forces. Extreme heat, extreme sorrow, complete happiness, are all despotic principles that reign over spaces devoid of production; they insist on being solitary; they stifle all that is not themselves. Vandenesse was not a woman, and none but women know the art of varying happiness; hence their coquetry, refusals, fears, quarrels, and the all-wise clever foolery with which they put in doubt the things that seemed to be without a cloud the night before. Men may weary by their constancy, but women never. Vandenesse was too thoroughly kind by nature to worry deliberately the woman he loved; on the contrary, he kept her in the bluest and least cloudy heaven of love. The problem of eternal beatitude is one of those whose solution is known only to God. Here, below, the sublimest poets have simply harassed their readers when attempting to picture paradise. Dante's reef was that of Vandenesse; all honor to such courage!

Felix's wife began to find monotony in an Eden so well arranged; the perfect happiness which the first woman found in her terrestrial paradise gave her at length a sort of nausea of sweet things, and made the countess wish, like Rivarol reading Florian, for a wolf in the fold. Such, judging by the history of ages, appears to be the meaning of that emblematic serpent to which Eve listened, in all probability, out of ennui. This deduction may seem a little venturesome to Protestants, who take the book of Genesis more seriously than the Jews themselves.

The situation of Madame de Vandenesse can, however, be explained without recourse to Biblical images. She felt in her soul an enormous power that was unemployed. Her happiness gave her no suffering; it rolled along without care or uneasiness; she was not afraid of losing it; each morning it shone upon her, with the same blue sky, the same smile, the same sweet words. That clear, still lake was unruffled by any breeze, even a zephyr; she would fain have seen a ripple on its glassy surface. Her desire had something so infantine about it that it ought to be excused; but society is not more indulgent than the God of Genesis. Madame de Vandenesse, having now become intelligently clever, was aware that such sentiments were not permissible, and she refrained from confiding them to her "dear little husband." Her genuine simplicity had not invented any other name for him; for one can't call up in cold blood that delightfully exaggerated language which love imparts to its victims in the midst of flames.

Vandenesse, glad of this adorable reserve, kept his wife, by deliberate calculations, in the temperate regions of conjugal affection. He never condescended to seek a reward or even an acknowledgment of the infinite pains which he gave himself; his wife thought his luxury and good taste her natural right, and she felt no gratitude for the fact that her pride and self-love had never suffered. It was thus in everything. Kindness has its mishaps; often it is attributed to temperament; people are seldom willing to recognize it as the secret effort of a noble soul.

About this period of her life, Madame Felix de Vandenesse had attained to a degree of worldly knowle-dge which enabled her to quit the insignificant role of a timid, listening, and observing super-numerary, - a part played, they say, for some time, by Giulia Grisi in the chorus at La Scala. The young countess now felt herself capable of attempting the part of prima-donna, and she did so on several occasions. To the great satisfaction of her husband, she began to mingle in conversations. Intelligent ideas and delicate observations put into her mind by her intercourse with her husband, made her remarked upon, and success emboldened her. Vandenesse, to whom the world admitted that his wife was beautiful, was delighted when the same assurance was given that she was clever and witty. On their return from a ball, concert, or rout where Marie had shone brilliantly, she would turn to her husband, as she took off her ornaments, and say, with a joyous, self-assured air, -

"Were you pleased with me this evening?"

The countess excited jealousies; among others that of her husband's sister, Madame de Listomere, who until now had patronized her, thinking that she protected a foil to her own merits. A countess, beautiful, witty and virtuous! - what a prey for the tongues of the world! Felix had broken with too many women, and too many women had broken with him, to leave them indifferent to his marriage. When these women beheld in Madame de Vandenesse a small woman with red hands, and rather awkward manner, saying little, and apparently not thinking much, they thought themselves sufficiently avenged. The disasters of July, 1830, supervened; society was dissolved for two years; the rich evaded the turmoil and left Paris either for foreign travel or for their estates in the country, and none of the salons reopened until 1833. When that time came, the faubourg Saint-Germain still sulked, but it held intercourse with a few houses, regarding them as neutral ground, - among others that of the Austrian ambassador, where the legitimist society and the new social world met together in the persons of their best representatives.

Attached by many ties of the heart and by gratitude to the exiled family, and strong in his personal convictions, Vandenesse did not consider himself obliged to imitate the silly behavior of his party. In times of danger, he had done his duty at the risk of his life; his fidelity had never been compromised, and he determined to take his wife into general society without fear of its becoming so. His former mistresses could scarcely recognize the bride they had thought so childish in the elegant, witty, and gentle countess, who now appeared in society with the exquisite manners of the highest female aristocracy. Mesdames d'Espard, de Manerville, and Lady Dudley, with others less known, felt the serpent waking up in the depths of their hearts; they heard the low hissings of angry pride; they were jealous of Felix's happiness, and would gladly have given their prettiest jewel to do him some harm; but instead of being hostile to the countess, these kind, ill-natured women surrounded her, showed her the utmost friendship, and praised her to me. Sufficiently aware of their intentions, Felix watched their relations with Marie, and warned her to distrust them. They all suspected the uneasiness of the count at their intimacy with his wife, and they redoubled their attentions and flatteries, so that they gave her an enormous vogue in society, to the great displeasure of her sister-in-law, the Marquise de Listomere, who could not understand it.

The Comtesse Felix de Vandenesse was cited as the most charming and the cleverest woman in Paris. Marie's other sister-in-law, the Marquise Charles de Vandenesse, was consumed with vexation at the confusion of names and the comparisons it sometimes brought about. Though the marquise was a handsome and clever woman, her rivals took delight in comparing her with her sister-in-law, with all the more point because the countess was a dozen years younger. These women knew very well what bitterness Marie's social vogue would bring into her intercourse with both of her sisters-in-law, who, in fact, became cold and disobliging in proportion to her triumph in society. She was thus surrounded by dangerous relations and intimate enemies.

Every one knows that French literature at that particular period was endeavoring to defend itself against an apathetic indifference (the result of the political drama) by producing works more or less Byronian, in which the only topics really discussed were conjugal delinquencies. Infringements of the marriage tie formed the staple of reviews, books, and dramas. This eternal subject grew more and more the fashion. The lover, that nightmare of husbands, was everywhere, except perhaps in homes, where, in point of fact, under the bourgeois regime, he was less seen than formerly. It is not when every one rushes to their window and cries "Thief!" and lights the streets, that robbers abound. It is true that during those years so fruitful of turmoil - urban, political, and moral - a few matrimonial catastrophes took place; but these were exceptional, and less observed than they would have been under the Restoration. Nevertheless, women talked a great deal together about books and the stage, then the two chief forms of poesy. The lover thus became one of their leading topics, - a being rare in point of act and much desired. The few affairs which were known gave rise to discussions, and these discussions were, as usually happens, carried on by immaculate women.

A fact worthy of remark is the aversion shown to such conversations by women who are enjoying some illicit happiness; they maintain before the eyes of the world a reserved, prudish, and even timid countenance; they seem to ask silence on the subject, or some condonation of their pleasure from society. When, on the contrary, a woman talks freely of such catastrophes, and seems to take pleasure in doing so, allowing herself to explain the emotions that justify the guilty parties, we may be sure that she herself is at the crossways of indecision, and does not know what road she might take.

During this winter, the Comtesse de Vandenesse heard the great voice of the social world roaring in her ears, and the wind of its stormy gusts blew round her. Her pretended friends, who maintained their reputations at the height of their rank and their positions, often produced in her presence the seductive idea of the lover; they cast into her soul certain ardent talk of love, the "mot d'enigme" which life propounds to woman, the grand passion, as Madame de Stael called it, - preaching by example. When the countess asked naively, in a small and select circle of these friends, what difference there was between a lover and a husband, all those who wished evil to Felix took care to reply in a way to pique her curiosity, or fire her imagination, or touch her heart, or interest her mind.

"Oh! my dear, we vegetate with a husband, but we live

with a lover," said her sister-in-law, the marquise.

"Marriage, my dear, is our purgatory; love is paradise," said Lady Dudley.

"Don't believe her," cried Mademoiselle des Touches; "it is hell."

"But a hell we like," remarked Madame de Rochefide. "There is often more pleasure in suffering than in happiness; look at the martyrs!"

"With a husband, my dear innocent, we live, as it were, in our own life; but to love, is to live in the life of another," said the Marquise d'Espard.

"A lover is forbidden fruit, and that to me, says all!" cried the pretty Moina de Saint-Heren, laughing.

When she was not at some diplomatic rout, or at a ball given by rich foreigners, like Lady Dudley or the Princesse Galathionne, the Comtesse de Vandenesse might be seen, after the Opera, at the houses of Madame d'Espard, the Marquise de Listomere, Mademoiselle des Touches, the Comtesse de Montcornet, or the Vicomtesse de Grandlieu, the only aristocratic houses then open; and never did she leave any one of them without some evil seed of the world being sown in her heart. She heard talk of completing her life, - a saying much in fashion in those days; of being comprehended, - another word to which women gave strange meanings. She often returned home uneasy, excited, curious, and thoughtful. She began to find something less, she hardly knew what, in her life; but she did not yet go so far as to think it lonely.

CHAPTER IV

A CELEBRATED MAN

The most amusing society, but also the most mixed, which Madame Felix de Vandenesse frequented, was that of the Comtesse de Montcornet, a charming little woman, who received illustrious artists, leading financial personages, distinguished writers; but only after subjecting them to so rigid an examination that the most exclusive aristocrat had nothing to fear in coming in contact with this second-class society. The loftiest pretensions were there respected.

During the winter of 1833, when society rallied after the revolution of July, some salons, notably those of Mesdames d'Espard and de Listomere, Mademoiselle des Touches, and the Duchesse de Grandlieu, had selected certain of the celebrities in art, science, literature, and politics, and received them. Society can lose nothing of its rights, and it must be amused. At a concert given by Madame de Montcornet toward the close of the winter of 1833, a man of rising fame in literature and politics appeared in her salon, brought there by one of the wittiest, but also one of the laziest writers of that epoch, Emile Blondet, celebrated behind closed doors, highly praised by journalists, but unknown beyond the barriers. Blondet himself was well aware of this; he indulged in no illusions, and, among his other witty and contemptuous sayings, he was wont to remark that fame is a poison good to take in little doses.

From the moment when the man we speak of, Raoul Nathan, after a long struggle, forced his way to the public gaze, he had put to profit the sudden infatuation for form manifested by those elegant descendants of the middle ages, jestingly called Young France. He assumed the singularities of a man of genius and enrolled himself among those adorers of art, whose intentions, let us say, were excellent; for surely nothing could be more ridiculous than the costume of Frenchmen in the nineteenth century, and nothing more courageous than an attempt to reform it. Raoul, let us do him this justice, presents in his person something fine, fantastic, and extraordinary, which needs a frame. His enemies, or his friends, they are about the same thing, agree that nothing could harmonize better with his mind than his outward form.

Raoul Nathan would, perhaps, be more singular if left to his natural self than he is with his various accompaniments. His worn and haggard face gives him an appearance of having fought with angels or devils; it bears some resemblance to that the German painters give to the dead Christ; countless signs of a constant struggle between failing human nature and the powers on high appear in it. But the lines in his hollow cheeks, the projections of his crooked, furrowed skull, the caverns around his eyes and behind his temples, show nothing weakly in his constitution. His hard membranes, his visible bones are the signs of remarkable solidity; and though his skin, discolored by excesses, clings to those bones as if dried there by inward fires, it nevertheless covers a most powerful structure. He is thin and tall. His long hair, always in disorder, is worn so for effect. This ill-combed, ill-made Byron has heron legs and stiffened knee-joints, an exaggerated stoop, hands with knotty muscles, firm as a crab's claws, and long, thin, wiry fingers. Raoul's eyes are Napoleonic, blue eyes, which pierce to the soul; his nose is crooked and very shrewd; his mouth charming, embellished with the whitest teeth that any woman could desire. There is fire and movement in the head, and genius on that brow. Raoul belongs to the small number of men who strike your mind as you pass them, and who, in a salon, make a luminous spot to which all eyes are attracted.

He makes himself remarked also by his "neglige," if we may borrow from Moliere the word which Eliante uses to express the want of personal neatness. His clothes always seem to have been twisted, frayed, and crumpled intent-ionally, in order to harmonize with his physiognomy. He keeps one of his hands habitually in the bosom of his waistcoat in the pose which Girodet's portrait of Monsieur de Chateaubriand has rendered famous; but less to imitate that great man (for he does not wish to resemble any one) than to rumple the over-smooth front of his shirt. His cravat is no sooner put on than it is twisted by the convulsive motions of his head, which are quick and abrupt, like those of a thoroughbred horse impatient of harness, and constantly tossing up its head to rid itself of bit and bridle. His long and pointed beard is neither combed, nor perfumed, nor brushed, nor trimmed, like those of the elegant young men of society; he lets it alone, to grow as it will. His hair, getting between the collar of his coat and his cravat, lies luxuriantly on his shoulders, and greases whatever spot it touches. His wiry, bony hands ignore a nailbrush and the luxury of lemon. Some of his cofeuilletonists declare that purifying waters seldom touch their calcined skin.

In short, the terrible Raoul is grotesque. His movements are jerky, as if produced by imperfect machinery; his gait rejects all idea of order, and proceeds by spasmodic zig-zags and sudden stoppages, which knock him violently against peaceable citizens on the streets and boulevards of Paris. His conversation, full of caustic humor, of bitter satire, follows the gait of his body; suddenly it abandons its tone of vengeance and turns sweet, poetic, consoling, gentle, without apparent reason; he falls into inexplicable silences, or turns somersets of wit, which at times are somewhat wearying. In society, he is boldly awkward, and exhibits a contempt for conventions and a critical air about things respected which makes him unpleasant to narrow minds, and also to those who strive to preserve the doctrines of old-fashioned, gentlemanly politeness; but for all that there is a sort of lawless originality about him which women do not dislike. Besides, to them, he is often most amiably courteous; he seems to take pleasure in making them forget his personal singularities, and thus obtains a victory over antipathies which flatters either his vanity, his self-love, or his pride.

"Why do you present yourself like that?" said the Marquise de Vandenesse one day.

"Pearls live in oyster-shells," he answered, conceitedly.

To another who asked him somewhat the same question, he replied, -

"If I were charming to all the world, how could I seem

better still to the one woman I wish to please?"

Raoul Nathan imports this same natural disorder (which he uses as a banner) into his intellectual life; and the attribute is not misleading. His talent is very much that of the poor girls who go about in bourgeois families to work by the day. He was first a critic, and a great critic; but he felt himself cheated in that vocation. His articles were equal to books, he said. The profits of theatrical work then allured him; but, incapable of the slow and steady application required for stage arrangement, he was forced to associate with himself a vaudevillist, du Bruel, who took his ideas, worked them over, and reduced them into those productive little pieces, full of wit, which are written expressly for actors and actresses. Between them, they had invented Florine, an actress now in vogue.

Humiliated by this association, which was that of the Siamese twins, Nathan had produced alone, at the Theatre-Francais, a serious drama, which fell with all the honors of war amid salvos of thundering articles. In his youth he had once before appeared at the great and noble Theatre-Francais in a splendid romantic play of the style of "Pinto," - a period when the classic reigned supreme. The Odeon was so violently agitated for three nights that the play was forbidden by the censor. This second piece was considered by many a masterpiece, and won him more real reputation than all his productive little pieces done with collaborators, - but only among a class to whom little attention is paid, that of connoisseurs and persons of true taste.

"Make another failure like that," said Emile Blondet, "and you'll be immortal."

But instead of continuing in that difficult path, Nathan had fallen, out of sheer necessity, into the powder and patches of eighteenth-century vaudeville, costume plays, and the reproduction, scenically, of successful novels.

Nevertheless, he passed for a great mind which had not said its last word. He had, moreover, attempted permanent literature, having published three novels, not to speak of several others which he kept in press like fish in a tank. One of these three books, the first (like that of many writers who can only make one real trip into literature), had obtained a very brilliant success. This work, imprudently placed in the front rank, this really artistic work he was never weary of calling the finest book of the period, the novel of the century.

Raoul complained bitterly of the exigencies of art. He was one of those who contributed most to bring all created work, pictures, statues, books, building under the single standard of Art. He had begun his career by committing a volume of verse, which won him a place in the pleiades of living poets; among these verses was a nebulous poem that was greatly admired. Forced by want of means to keep on producing, he went from the theatre to the press, and from the press to the theatre, dissipating and scattering his talent, but believing always in his vein. His fame was therefore not unpublished like that of so many great minds in extremity, who sustain themselves only by the thought of work to be done.

Nathan resembled a man of genius; and had he marched to the scaffold, as he sometimes wished he could have done, he might have struck his brow with the famous action of Andre Chenier. Seized with political ambition on seeing the rise to power of a dozen authors, professors, metaphysicians, and historians, who encrusted themselves, so to speak, upon the machine during the turmoils of 1830 and 1833, he regretted that he had not spent his time on political instead of literary articles. He thought himself superior to all those parvenus, whose success inspired him with consuming jealousy. He belonged to the class of minds ambitious of everything, capable of all things, from whom success is, as it were, stolen; who go their way dashing at a hundred luminous points, and settling upon none, exhausting at last the good-will of others.

At this particular time he was going from Saint-Simonism into republicanism, to return, very likely, to ministeri-alism. He looked for a bone to gnaw in all corners, searching for a safe place where he could bark secure from kicks and make himself feared. But he had the mortification of finding he was held to be of no account by de Marsay, then at the head of the government, who had no consideration whatever for authors, among whom he did not find what Richelieu called a consecutive mind, or more correctly, continuity of ideas; he counted as any minister would have done on the constant embarrassment of Raoul's business affairs. Sooner or later, necessity would bring him to accept conditions instead of imposing them.

The real, but carefully concealed character of Raoul Nathan is of a piece with his public career. He is a comedian in good faith, selfish as if the State were himself, and a very clever orator. No one knows better how to play off sentiments, glory in false grandeurs, deck himself with moral beauty, do honor to his nature in language, and pose like Alceste while behaving like

Philinte. His egotism trots along protected by this cardboard armor, and often almost reaches the end he seeks. Lazy to a superlative degree, he does nothing, however, until he is prodded by the bayonets of need. He is incapable of continued labor applied to the creation of a work; but, in a paroxysm of rage caused by wounded vanity, or in a crisis brought on by creditors, he leaps the Eurotas and attains to some great triumph of his intellect. After which, weary, and surprised at having created anything, he drops back into the marasmus of Parisian dissipation; wants become formidable; he has no strength to face them; and then he comes down from his pedestal and compromises.

Influenced by a false idea of his grandeur and of his future, - the measure of which he reckons on the noble success of one of his former comrades, one of the few great talents brought to light by the revolution of July, - he allows himself, in order to get out of his embarrassments, certain laxities of principle with persons who are friendly to him, - laxities which never come to the surface, but are buried in private life, where no one ever mentions or complains of them. The shallowness of his heart, the impurity of his hand, which clasps that of all vices, all evils, all treacheries, all opinions, have made him as inviolable as a constitutional king. Venial sins, which excite a hue and cry against a man of high character, are thought nothing of in him; the world hastens to excuse them. Men who might otherwise be inclined to despise him shake hands with him, fearing that the day may come when they will need him. He has, in fact, so many friends that he wishes for enemies.

Judged from a literary point of view, Nathan lacks

style and cultivation. Like most young men, ambitious of literary fame, he disgorges to-day what he acquired yesterday. He has neither the time nor the patience to write carefully; he does not observe, but he listens. Incapable of constructing a vigorously framed plot, he sometimes makes up for it by the impetuous ardor of his drawing. He "does passion," to use a term of the literary argot; but instead of awaking ideas, his heroes are simply enlarged individualities, who excite only fugitive sympathies; they are not connected with any of the great interests of life, and consequently they represent nothing. Nevertheless, Nathan maintains his ground by the quickness of his mind, by those lucky hits which billiard-players call a "good stroke." He is the cleverest shot at ideas on the fly in all Paris. His fecundity is not his own, but that of his epoch; he lives on chance events, and to control them he distorts their meaning. In short, he is not *true*; his presentation is false; in him, as Comte Felix said, is the born juggler. Moreover, his pen gets its ink in the boudoir of an actress.

Raoul Nathan is a fair type of the Parisian literary youth of the day, with its false grandeurs and its real misery. He represents that youth by his incomplete beauties and his headlong falls, by the turbulent torrent of his existence, with its sudden reverses and its unhoped-for triumphs. He is truly the child of a century consumed with envy, - a century with a thousand rivalries lurking under many a system, which nourish to their own profit that hydra of anarchy which wants wealth without toil, fame without talent, success without effort, but whose vices force it, after much rebellion and many skirmishes, to accept the budget under the powers that be. When so many young ambitions, starting on foot, give one another rendezvous at the same point, there is always contention of wills, extreme wretchedness, bitter struggles. In this dreadful battle, selfishness, the most overbearing or the most adroit selfishness, gains the victory; and it is envied and applauded in spite, as Moliere said, of outcries, and we all know it.

When, in his capacity as enemy to the new dynasty, Raoul was introduced in the salon of Madame de Montcornet, his apparent grandeurs were flourishing. He was accepted as the political critic of the de Marsays, the Rastignacs, and the Roche-Hugons, who had stepped into power. Emile Blondet, the victim of incurable hesitation and of his innate repugnance to any action that concerned only himself, continued his trade of scoffer, took sides with no one, and kept well with all. He was friendly with Raoul, friendly with Rastignac, friendly with Montcornet.

"You are a political triangle," said de Marsay, laughing, when they met at the Opera. "That geometric form, my dear fellow, belongs only to the Deity, who has nothing to do; ambitious men ought to follow curved lines, the shortest road in politics."

Seen from a distance, Raoul Nathan was a very fine meteor. Fashion accepted his ways and his appearance. His borrowed republicanism gave him, for the time being, that Jansenist harshness assumed by the defenders of the popular cause, while they inwardly scoff at it, - a quality not without charm in the eyes of women. Women like to perform prodigies, break rocks, and soften natures which seem of iron.

Raoul's moral costume was therefore in keeping with his clothes. He was fitted to be what he became to the

Honore de Balzac

Eve who was bored in her paradise in the rue du Rocher, - the fascinating serpent, the fine talker with magnetic eyes and harmonious motions who tempted the first woman. No sooner had the Comtesse Marie laid eyes on Raoul than she felt an inward emotion, the violence of which caused her a species of terror. The glance of that fraudulent great man exercised a physical influence upon her, which quivered in her very heart, and troubled it. But the trouble was pleasure. The purple mantle which celebrity had draped for a moment round Nathan's shoulders dazzled the ingenuous young woman. When tea was served, she rose from her seat among a knot of talking women, where she had been striving to see and hear that extraordinary being. Her silence and absorption were noticed by her false friends.

The countess approached the divan in the centre of the room, where Raoul was perorating. She stood there with her arm in that of Madame Octave de Camp, an excellent woman, who kept the secret of the involuntary trembling by which these violent emotions betrayed themselves. Though the eyes of a captivated woman are apt to shed wonderful sweetness, Raoul was too occupied at that moment in letting off fireworks, too absorbed in his epigrams going up like rockets (in the midst of which were flaming portraits drawn in lines of fire) to notice the naive admiration of one little Eve concealed in a group of women. Marie's curiosity - like that which would undoubtedly precipitate all Paris into the Jardin des Plantes to see a unicorn, if such an animal could be found in those mountains of the moon, still virgin of the tread of Europeans - intoxicates a secondary mind as much as it saddens great ones; but Raoul was enchanted by it; although he was then too anxious to secure all women to care very much for one alone.

"Take care, my dear," said Marie's kind and gracious companion in her ear, "and go home."

The countess looked at her husband to ask for his arm with one of those glances which husbands do not always understand. Felix did so, and took her home.

"My dear friend," said Madame d'Espard in Raoul's ear, "you are a lucky fellow. You have made more than one conquest to-night, and among them that of the charming woman who has just left us so abruptly."

"Do you know what the Marquise d'Espard meant by that?" said Raoul to Rastignac, when they happened to be comparatively alone between one and two o'clock in the morning.

"I am told that the Comtesse de Vandenesse has taken a violent fancy to you. You are not to be pitied!" said Rastignac.

"I did not see her," said Raoul.

"Oh! but you will see her, you scamp!" cried Emile Blondet, who was standing by. "Lady Dudley is going to ask you to her grand ball, that you may meet the pretty countess."

Raoul and Blondet went off with Rastignac, who offered them his carriage. All three laughed at the combination of an eclectic under-secretary of State, a ferocious republican, and a political atheist.

"Suppose we sup at the expense of the present order of

things?" said Blondet, who would fain recall suppers to fashion.

Rastignac took them to Very's, sent away his carriage, and all three sat down to table to analyze society with Rabelaisian laughs. During the supper, Rastignac and Blondet advised their provisional enemy not to neglect such a capital chance of advancement as the one now offered to him. The two "roues" gave him, in fine satirical style, the history of Madame Felix de Vandenesse; they drove the scalpel of epigram and the sharp points of much good wit into that innocent girlhood and happy marriage. Blondet congratulated Raoul on encountering a woman guilty of nothing worse so far than horrible drawings in red chalk, attenuated water-colors, slippers embroidered for a husband, sonatas executed with the best intentions, - a girl tied to her mother's apron-strings till she was eighteen, trussed for religious practices, seasoned by Vandenesse, and cooked to a point by marriage. At the third bottle of champagne, Raoul unbosomed himself as he had never done before in his life.

"My friends," he said, "you know my relations with Florine; you also know my life, and you will not be surprised to hear me say that I am absolutely ignorant of what a countess's love may be like. I have often felt mortified that I, a poet, could not give myself a Beatrice, a Laura, except in poetry. A pure and noble woman is like an unstained conscience, - she represents us to ourselves under a noble form. Elsewhere we may soil ourselves, but with her we are always proud, lofty, and immaculate. Elsewhere we lead ill-regulated lives; with her we breathe the calm, the freshness, the verdure of an oasis -"

"Go on, go on, my dear fellow!" cried Rastignac; "twang that fourth string with the prayer in 'Moses' like Paganini."

Raoul remained silent, with fixed eyes, apparently musing.

"This wretched ministerial apprentice does not understand me," he said, after a moment's silence.

So, while the poor Eve in the rue du Rocher went to bed in the sheets of shame, frightened at the pleasure with which she had listened to that sham great poet, these three bold minds were trampling with jests over the tender flowers of her dawning love. Ah! if women only knew the cynical tone that such men, so humble, so fawning in their presence, take behind their backs! how they sneer at what they say they adore! Fresh, pure, gracious being, how the scoffing jester disrobes and analyzes her! but, even so, the more she loses veils, the more her beauty shines.

Marie was at this moment comparing Raoul and Felix, without imagining the danger there might be for her in such comparisons. Nothing could present a greater contrast than the disorderly, vigorous Raoul to Felix de Vandenesse, who cared for his person like a dainty woman, wore well-fitting clothes, had a charming "desinvoltura," and was a votary of English nicety, to which, in earlier days, Lady Dudley had trained him. Marie, as a good and pious woman, soon forbade herself even to think of Raoul, and considered that she was a monster of ingratitude for making the comparison.

"What do you think of Raoul Nathan?" she asked her

husband the next day at breakfast.

"He is something of a charlatan," replied Felix; "one of those volcanoes who are easily calmed down with a little gold-dust. Madame de Montcornet makes a mistake in admitting him."

This answer annoyed Marie, all the more because Felix supported his opinion with certain facts, relating what he knew of Raoul Nathan's life, - a precarious existence mixed up with a popular actress.

"If the man has genius," he said in conclusion, "he certainly has neither the constancy nor the patience which sanctifies it, and makes it a thing divine. He endeavors to impose on the world by placing himself on a level which he does nothing to maintain. True talent, pains-taking and honorable talent does not act thus. Men who possess such talent follow their path courageously; they accept its pains and penalties, and don't cover them with tinsel."

A woman's thought is endowed with incredible elasticity. When she receives a knockdown blow, she bends, seems crushed, and then renews her natural shape in a given time.

"Felix is no doubt right," thought she.

But three days later she was once more thinking of the serpent, recalled to him by that singular emotion, painful and yet sweet, which the first sight of Raoul had given her. The count and countess went to Lady Dudley's grand ball, where, by the bye, de Marsay appeared in society for the last time. He died about two months later, leaving the reputation of a great statesman, because, as Blondet remarked, he was incomprehensible.

Vandenesse and his wife again met Raoul Nathan at this ball, which was remarkable for the meeting of several personages of the political drama, who were not a little astonished to find themselves together. It was one of the first solemnities of the great world. The salons presented a magnificent spectacle to the eye, - flowers, diamonds, and brilliant head-dresses; all jewel-boxes emptied; all resources of the toilet put under contribution. The ball-room might be compared to one of those choice conservatories where rich horticulturists collect the most superb rarities, - same brilliancy, same delicacy of texture. On all sides white or tinted gauzes like the wings of the airiest dragon-fly, crepes, laces, blondes, and tulles, varied as the fantasies of entomological nature; dentelled, waved, and scalloped; spider's webs of gold and silver; mists of silk embroidered by fairy fingers; plumes colored by the fire of the tropics drooping from haughty heads; pearls twined in braided hair; shot or ribbed or brocaded silks, as though the genius of arabesque had presided over French manufactures, - all this luxury was in harmony with the beauties collected there as if to realize a "Keepsake." The eye received there an impression of the whitest shoulders, some amber-tinted, others so polished as to seem colandered, some dewy, some plump and satiny, as though Rubens had prepared their flesh; in short, all shades known to man in white. Here were eyes sparkling like onyx or turquoise fringed with dark lashes; faces of varied outline presenting the most graceful types of many lands; foreheads noble and majestic, or softly rounded, as if thought ruled, or flat, as if resistant will reigned there unconquered; beautiful bosoms swelling, as

George IV. admired them, or widely parted after the fashion of the eighteenth century, or pressed together, as Louis XV. required; some shown boldly, without veils, others covered by those charming pleated chemisettes which Raffaelle painted. The prettiest feet pointed for the dance, the slimmest waists encircled in the waltz, stimulated the gaze of the most indifferent person present. The murmur of sweet voices, the rustle of gowns, the cadence of the dance, the whir of the waltz harmoniously accompanied the music. A fairy's wand seemed to have commanded this dazzling revelry, this melody of perfumes, these iridescent lights glittering from crystal chandeliers or sparkling in candelabra. This assemblage of the prettiest women in their prettiest dresses stood out upon a gloomy background of men in black coats, among whom the eye remarked the elegant, delicate, and correctly drawn profile of nobles, the ruddy beards and grave faces of Englishmen, and the more gracious faces of the French aristocracy. All the orders of Europe glittered on the breasts or hung from the necks of these men.

Examining this society carefully, it was seen to present not only the brilliant tones and colors and outward adornment, but to have a soul, - it lived, it felt, it thought. Hidden passions gave it a physiognomy; mischievous or malignant looks were exchanged; fair and giddy girls betrayed desires; jealous women told each other scandals behind their fans, or paid exaggerated compliments. Society, anointed, curled, and perfumed, gave itself up to social gaiety which went to the brain like a heady liquor. It seemed as if from all foreheads, as well as from all hearts, ideas and sentiments were exhaling, which presently condensed and reacted in a volume on the coldest persons present, and excited them. At the most animated moment of this intoxicating party, in a corner of a gilded salon where certain bankers, ambassadors, and the immoral old English earl, Lord Dudley, were playing cards, Madame Felix de Vandenesse was irresistibly drawn to converse with Raoul Nathan. Possibly she yielded to that ball-intoxication which sometimes wrings avowals from the most discreet.

At sight of such a fete, and the splendors of a world in which he had never before appeared, Nathan was stirred to the soul by fresh ambition. Seeing Rastignac, whose younger brother had just been made bishop at twenty-seven years of age, and whose brother-in-law, Martial de la Roche-Hugon, was a minister, and who himself was under-secretary of State, and about to marry, rumor said, the only daughter of the Baron de Nucingen, - a girl with an illimitable "dot"; seeing, moreover, in the diplomatic body an obscure writer whom he had formerly known translating articles in foreign journals for a newspaper turned dynastic since 1830, also professors now made peers of France, - he felt with anguish that he was left behind on a bad road by advocating the overthrow of this new aristocracy of lucky talent, of cleverness crowned by success, and of real merit. Even Blondet, so unfortunate, so used by others in journalism, but so welcomed here, who could, if he liked, enter a career of public service through the influence of Madame de Montcornet, seemed to Nathan's eyes a striking example of the power of social relations. Secretly, in his heart, he resolved to play the game of political opinions, like de Marsay, Rastignac, Blondet, Talleyrand, the leader of this set of men; to rely on facts only, turn them to his own profit, regard his system as a weapon, and not interfere with a society so well constituted, so shrewd, so natural.

"My influence," he thought, "will depend on the influence of some woman belonging to this class of society."

With this thought in his mind, conceived by the flame of this frenzied desire, he fell upon the Comtesse de Vandenesse like a hawk on its prey. That charming young woman in her head-dress of marabouts, which produced the delightful "flou" of the paintings of Lawrence and harmonized well with her gentle nature, was penetrated through and through by the foaming vigor of this poet wild with ambition. Lady Dudley, whom nothing escaped, aided this tete-a-tete by throwing the Comte de Vandenesse with Madame de Manerville. Strong in her former ascendancy over him, Natalie de Manerville amused herself by leading Felix into the mazes of a quarrel of witty teasing, blushing half-confidences, regrets coyly flung like flowers at his feet, recriminations in which she excused herself for the sole purpose of being put in the wrong.

These former lovers were speaking to each other for the first time since their rupture; and while her husband's former love was stirring the embers to see if a spark were yet alive, Madame Felix de Vandenesse was undergoing those violent palpitations which a woman feels at the certainty of doing wrong, and stepping on forbidden ground, - emotions that are not without charm, and which awaken various dormant faculties. Women are fond of using Bluebeard's bloody key, that fine mythological idea for which we are indebted to Perrault.

The dramatist - who knew his Shakespeare - displayed his wretchedness, related his struggle with men and things, made his hearer aware of his baseless grandeur, his unrecognized political genius, his life without noble affections. Without saying a single definite word, he contrived to suggest to this charming woman that she should play the noble part of Rebecca in Ivanhoe, and love and protect him. It was all, of course, in the ethereal regions of sentiment. Forget-me-nots are not more blue, lilies not more white than the images, thoughts, and radiantly illumined brow of this accomplished artist, who was likely to send his conversation to a publisher. He played his part of reptile to this poor Eve so cleverly, he made the fatal bloom of the apple so dazzling to her eyes, that Marie left the ball-room filled with that species of remorse which resembles hope, flattered in all her vanities, stirred to every corner of her heart, caught by her own virtues, allured by her native pity for misfortune.

Perhaps Madame de Manerville had taken Vandenesse into the salon where his wife was talking with Nathan; perhaps he had come there himself to fetch Marie, and take her home; perhaps his conversation with his former flame had awakened slumbering griefs; certain it is that when his wife took his arm to leave the ball-room, she saw that his face was sad and his look serious. The countess wondered if he was displeased with her. No sooner were they seated in the carriage than she turned to Felix and said, with a mischievous smile, -

"Did not I see you talking half the evening with Madame de Manerville?"

Felix was not out of the tangled paths into which his wife had led him by this charming little quarrel, when the carriage turned into their court-yard. This was Marie's first artifice dictated by her new emotion; and she even took pleasure in triumphing over a man who, until then, had seemed to her so superior.

CHAPTER V

FLORINE

Between the rue Basse-du-Rempart and the rue Neuve-des-Mathurins, Raoul had, on the third floor of an ugly and narrow house, in the Passage Sandrie, a poor enough lodging, cold and bare, where he lived ostensibly for the general public, for literary neophytes, and for his creditors, duns, and other annoying persons whom he kept on the threshold of private life. His real home, his fine existence, his presentation of himself before his friends, was in the house of Mademoiselle Florine, a second-class comedy actress, where, for ten years, the said friends, journalists, certain authors, and writers in general disported themselves in the society of equally illustrious actresses. For ten years Raoul had attached himself so closely to this woman that he passed more than half his life with her; he took all his meals at her house unless he had some friend to invite, or an invitation to dinner elsewhere.

To consummate corruption, Florine added a lively wit, which intercourse with artists had developed and practice sharpened day by day. Wit is thought to be a quality rare in comedians. It is so natural to suppose that persons who spend their lives in showing things on the outside have nothing within. But if we reflect on the small number of actors and actresses who live in each century, and also on how many dramatic authors and fascinating women this population has supplied relatively to its numbers, it is allowable to refute that opinion, which rests, and apparently will rest forever, on a criticism made against dramatic artists, - namely, that their personal sentiments are destroyed by the plastic presentation of passions; whereas, in fact, they put into their art only their gifts of mind, memory, and imagination. Great artists are beings who, to quote Napoleon, can cut off at will the connection which Nature has put between the senses and thought. Moliere and Talma, in their old age, were more in love than ordinary men in all their lives.

Accustomed to listen to journalists, who guess at most things, putting two and two together, to writers, who foresee and tell all that they see; accustomed also to the ways of certain political personages, who watched one another in her house, and profited by all admissions, Florine presented in her own person a mixture of devil and angel, which made her peculiarly fitted to receive these roues. They delighted in her cool self-possession; her anomalies of mind and heart entertained them prodigiously. Her house, enriched by gallant tributes, displayed the exaggerated magnificence of women who, caring little about the cost of things, care only for the things themselves, and give them the value of their own caprices, - women who will break a fan or a smelling-bottle fit for queens in a moment of passion, and scream with rage if a servant breaks a ten-franc saucer from which their poodle drinks.

Florine's dining-room, filled with her most distinguished offerings, will give a fair idea of this pell-mell of regal and fantastic luxury. Throughout, even on the ceilings, it was panelled in oak, picked out, here and there, by dead-gold lines. These panels were framed in relief with figures of children playing with fantastic animals, among which the light danced and floated, touching here a sketch by Bixiou, that maker of caricatures, there the cast of an angel holding a vessel of holy water (presented by Francois Souchet), farther on a coquettish painting of Joseph Bridau, a gloomy picture of a Spanish alchemist by Hippolyte Schinner, an autograph of Lord Byron to Lady Caroline Lamb, framed in carved ebony, while, hanging opposite as a species of pendant, was a letter from Napoleon to Josephine. All these things were placed about without the slightest symmetry, but with almost imperceptible art. On the chimney-piece, of exquisitely carved oak, there was nothing except a strange, evidently Florentine, ivory statuette attributed to Michael Angelo, representing Pan discovering a woman under the skin of a young shepherd, the original of which is in the royal palace of Vienna. On either side were candelabra of Renaissance design. A clock, by Boule, on a tortoise-shell stand, inlaid with brass, sparkled in the centre of one panel between two statuettes, undoubtedly obtained from the demolition of some abbey. In the corners of the room, on pedestals, were lamps of royal magnificence, as to which a manufacturer had made strong remonstrance against adapting his lamps to Japanese vases. On a marvellous sideboard was displayed a service of silver plate, the gift of an English lord, also porcelains in high relief; in short, the luxury of an actress who has no other property than her furniture.

The bedroom, all in violet, was a dream that Florine had indulged from her debut, the chief features of which were curtains of violet velvet lined with white silk, and looped over tulle; a ceiling of white cashmere with violet satin rays, an ermine carpet beside the bed; in the bed, the curtains of which resembled a lily turned upside down was a lantern by which to read the newspaper plaudits or criticisms before they appeared in the morning. A yellow salon, its effect heightened by trimmings of the color of Florentine bronze, was in harmony with the rest of these magnificences, a further description of which would make our pages resemble the posters of an auction sale. To find comparisons for all these fine things, it would be necessary to go to a certain house that was almost next door, belonging to a Rothschild.

Sophie Grignault, surnamed Florine by a form of baptism common in theatres, had made her first appearances, in spite of her beauty, on very inferior boards. Her success and her money she owed to Raoul Nathan. This association of their two fates, usual enough in the dramatic and literary world, did no harm to Raoul, who kept up the outward conventions of a man of the world. Moreover, Florine's actual means were precarious; her revenues came from her salary and her leaves of absence, and barely sufficed for her dress and her household expenses. Nathan gave her certain perquisites which he managed to levy as critic on several of the new enterprises of industrial art. But although he was always gallant and protecting towards her, that protection had nothing regular or solid about it.

This uncertainty, and this life on a bough, as it were, did not alarm Florine; she believed in her talent, and she believed in her beauty. Her robust faith was somewhat comical to those who heard her staking her future upon it, when remonstrances were made to her.

"I can have income enough when I please," she was wont to say; "I have invested fifty francs on the Grand-livre."

No one could ever understand how it happened that Florine, handsome as she was, had remained in obscurity for seven years; but the fact is, Florine was enrolled as a supernumerary at thirteen years of age, and made her debut two years later at an obscure boulevard theatre. At fifteen, neither beauty nor talent exist; a woman is simply all promise.

She was now twenty-eight, - the age at which the beauties of a French woman are in their glory. Painters particularly admired the lustre of her white shoulders, tinted with olive tones about the nape of the neck, and wonderfully firm and polished, so that the light shimmered over them as it does on watered silk. When she turned her head, superb folds formed about her neck, the admiration of sculptors. She carried on this triumphant neck the small head of a Roman empress, the delicate, round, and self-willed head of Pompeia, with features of elegant correctness, and the smooth forehead of a woman who drives all care away and all reflection, who yields easily, but is capable of balking like a mule, and incapable at such times of listening to reason. That forehead, turned, as it were, with one cut of the chisel, brought out the beauty of the golden hair, which was raised in front, after the Roman fashion, in two equal masses, and twisted up behind the head to prolong the line of the neck, and enhance that whiteness by its beautiful color. Black and delicate eyebrows, drawn by a Chinese brush, encircled the soft eyelids, which were threaded with rosy fibres. The pupils of the eyes, extremely bright, though striped with brown rays, gave to her glance the cruel fixity of a beast of prey, and betrayed the cold maliciousness of the courtesan. The eyes were gray, fringed with black lashes, - a charming contrast, which made their expression of calm and contemplative voluptuousness the more observable; the circle round the eyes showed marks of fatigue, but the artistic manner in which she could turn her eyeballs, right and left, or up and down, to observe, or seem to mediate, the way in which she could hold them fixed, casting out their vivid fire without moving her head, without taking from her face its absolute immovability (a manoeuvre learned upon the stage), and the vivacity of their glance, as she looked about a theatre in search of a friend, made her eyes the most terrible, also the softest, in short, the most extraordinary eyes in the world. Rouge had destroyed by this time the diaphanous tints of her cheeks, the flesh of which was still delicate; but although she could no longer blush or turn pale, she had a thin nose with rosy, passionate nostrils, made to express irony, - the mocking irony of Moliere's women-servants. Her sensual mouth, expressive of sarcasm and love of dissipation, was adorned with a deep furrow that united the upper lip with the nose. Her chin, white and rather fat, betrayed the violence of passion. Her hands and arms were worthy of a sovereign.

But she had one ineradicable sign of low birth, - her foot was short and fat. No inherited quality ever caused greater distress. Florine had tried everything, short of amputation, to get rid of it. The feet were obstinate, like the Breton race from which she came; they resisted all treatment. Florine now wore long boots stuffed with cotton, to give length, and the semblance of an instep. Her figure was of medium height, threatened with corpulence, but still well-balanced, and well-made.

Morally, she was an adept in all the attitudinizing, quarrelling, alluring, and cajoling of her business; and she gave to those actions a savor of their own by playing childlike innocence, and slipping in among her artless speeches philosophical malignities. Apparently ignorant and giddy, she was very strong on money-matters and commercial law, - for the reason that she had gone through so much misery before attaining to her present precarious success. She had come down, story by story, from the garret to the first floor, through so many vicissitudes! She knew life, from that which begins in Brie cheese and ends at pineapples; from that which cooks and washes in the corner of a garret on an earthenware stove, to that which convokes the tribes of pot-bellied chefs and saucemakers. She had lived on credit and not killed it; she was ignorant of nothing that honest women ignore; she spoke all languages: she was one of the populace by experience; she was noble by beauty and physical distinction. Suspicious as a spy, or a judge, or an old statesman, she was difficult to impose upon, and therefore the more able to see clearly into most matters. She knew the ways of managing tradespeople, and how to evade their snares, and she was quite as well versed in the prices of things as a public appraiser. To see her lying on her sofa, like a young bride, fresh and white, holding her part in her hand and learning it, you would have thought her a child of sixteen, ingenuous, ignorant, and weak, with no other artifice about her but her innocence. Let a creditor contrive to enter, and she was up like a startled fawn, and swearing a good round oath.

"Hey! my good fellow; your insolence is too dear an interest on the money I owe you," she would say. "I am sick of seeing you. Send the sheriff here; I'd prefer him to your silly face."

Florine gave charming dinners, concerts, and well-attended soirees, where play ran high. Her female friends were all handsome; no old woman had ever appeared within her precincts. She was not jealous; in fact, she would have thought jealousy an admission of inferiority. She had known Coralie and La Torpille in their lifetimes, and now knew Tullia, Euphrasie, Aquilina, Madame du Val-Noble, Mariette, - those women who pass through Paris like gossamer through the atmosphere, without our knowing where they go nor whence they came; to-day queens, to-morrow slaves. She also knew the actresses, her rivals, and all the prima-donnas; in short, that whole exceptional feminine society, so kindly, so graceful in its easy "sans-souci," which absorbs into its own Bohemian life all who allow themselves to be caught in the frantic whirl of its gay spirits, its eager abandonment, and its contemptuous indifference to the future.

Though this Bohemian life displayed itself in her house in tumultuous disorder, amid the laughter of artists of every description, the queen of the revels had ten fingers on which she knew better how to count than any of her guests. In that house secret saturnalias of literature and art, politics and finance were carried on; there, desire reigned a sovereign; there, caprice and fancy were as sacred as honor and virtue to a bourgeoise; thither came Blondet, Finot, Etienne Lousteau, Vernou the feuilletonist, Couture, Bixiou, Rastignac in his earlier days, Claude Vignon the critic, Nucingen the banker, du Tillet, Conti the composer, - in short, that whole devil-may-care legion of selfish materialists of all kinds; friends of Florine and of the singers, actresses and "danseuses" collected about her. They all hated or liked one another according to circumstances.

This Bohemian resort, to which celebrity was the only ticket of admission, was a Hades of the mind, the galleys of the intellect. No one could enter there without having legally conquered fortune, done ten years of misery, strangled two or three passions, acquired some celebrity, either by books or waistcoats, by dramas or fine equipages; plots were hatched there, means of making fortune scrutinized, all things were discussed and weighed. But every man, on leaving it, resumed the livery of his own opinions; there he could, without compromising himself, criticise his own party, admit the knowledge and good play of his adversaries, formulate thoughts that no one admits thinking, - in short, say all, as if ready to do all. Paris is the only place in the world where such eclectic houses exist; where all tastes, all vices, all opinions are received under decent guise. Therefore it is not yet certain that Florine will remain to the end of her career a second-class actress.

Florine's life was by no means an idle one, or a life to be envied. Many persons, misled by the magnificent pedestal that the stage gives to a woman, suppose her in the midst of a perpetual carnival. In the dark recesses of a porter's lodge, beneath the tiles of an attic roof, many a poor girl dreams, on returning from the theatre, of pearls and diamonds, gold-embroidered gowns and sumptuous girdles; she fancies herself adored, applauded, courted; but little she knows of that treadmill life, in which the actress is forced to rehearsals under pain of fines, to the reading of new pieces, to the constant study of new roles. At each representation Florine changes her dress at least two or three times; often she comes home exhausted and half-dead; but before she can rest, she must wash off with various cosmetics the white and the red she has applied, and clean all the powder from her hair, if she has played a part from the eighteenth century. She scarcely has time for food. When she plays, an actress can live no life of her own; she can neither dress, nor eat, nor talk. Florine often has no time to sup. On returning from a play, which lasts, in these days, till after midnight, she does not get to bed before two in the morning; but she must rise early to study her part, order her dresses, try them on, breakfast, read her love-letters, answer them, discuss with the leader of the "claque" the place for the plaudits, pay for the triumphs of the last month in solid cash, and bespeak those of the month ahead. In the days of Saint-Genest, the canonized comedian who fulfilled his duties in a pious manner and wore a hair shirt, we must suppose that an actor's life did not demand this incessant activity. Sometimes Florine, seized with a bourgeois desire to get out into the country and gather flowers, pretends to the manager that she is ill.

But even these mechanical operations are nothing in comparison with the intrigues to be carried on, the pains of wounded vanity to be endured, - preferences shown by authors, parts taken away or given to others, exactions of the male actors, spite of rivals, naggings of the stage manager, struggles with journalists; all of which require another twelve hours to the day. But even so far, nothing has been said of the art of acting, the expression of passion, the practice of positions and gesture, the minute care and watchfulness required on the stage, where a thousand opera-glasses are ready to detect a flaw, - labors which consumed the life and thought of Talma, Lekain, Baron, Contat, Clairon, Champmesle. In these infernal "coulisses" self-love has no sex; the artist who triumphs, be it man or woman, has all the other men and women against him or her. Then, as to money, however many engagements Florine may have, her salary does not cover the costs of her stage toilet, which, in addition to its costumes, requires an immense variety of long gloves, shoes, and frippery; and all this exclusive of her personal clothing. The first third of such a life is spent in struggling and imploring; the next third, in getting a foothold; the last third, in defending it. If happiness is frantically grasped, it is because it is so rare, so long desired, and found at last only amid the odious fictitious pleasures and smiles of such a life.

As for Florine, Raoul's power in the press was like a protecting sceptre; he spared her many cares and anxieties; she clung to him less as a lover than a prop; she took care of him like a father, she deceived him like a husband; but she would readily have sacrificed all she had to him. Raoul could, and did do everything for her vanity as an actress, for the peace of her self-love, and for her future on the stage. Without the intervention of a successful author, there is no successful actress; Champmesle was due to Racine, like Mars to Monvel and Andrieux. Florine could do nothing in return for Raoul, though she would gladly have been useful and necessary to him. She reckoned on the charms of habit to keep him by her; she was always ready to open her salons and display the luxury of her dinners and suppers for his friends, and to further his projects. She desired to be for him what Madame de Pompadour was to Louis XV. All actresses envied Florine's position, and some journalists envied that of Raoul.

Those to whom the inclination of the human mind towards chance, opposition, and contrasts is known, will readily understand that after ten years of this lawless Bohemian life, full of ups and downs, of fetes and sheriffs, of orgies and forced sobrieties, Raoul was attracted to the idea of another love, - to the gentle, harmonious house and presence of a great lady, just as the Comtesse Felix instinctively desired to introduce the torture of great emotions into a life made monotonous by happiness. This law of life is the law of all arts, which exist only by contrasts. A work done without this incentive is the loftiest expression of genius, just as the cloister is the highest expression of the Christian life.

On returning to his lodging from Lady Dudley's ball, Raoul found a note from Florine, brought by her maid, which an invincible sleepiness prevented him from reading at that moment. He fell asleep, dreaming of a gentle love that his life had so far lacked. Some hours later he opened the note, and found in it important news, which neither Rastignac nor de Marsay had allowed to transpire. The indiscretion of a member of the government had revealed to the actress the coming dissolution of the Chamber after the present session. Raoul instantly went to Florine's house and sent for Blondet. In the actress's boudoir, with their feet on the fender, Emile and Raoul analyzed the political situation of France in 1834. On which side lay the best chance of fortune? They reviewed all parties and all shades of party, - pure republicans, presiding republicans, republicans without a republic, constitutionals without a dynasty, ministerial conservatives, ministerial absolutists; also the Right, the aristocratic Right, the legitimist, henriquinquist Right, and the carlest Right. Between the party of resistance and that of action there was no discussion; they might as well have hesitated between life and death.

At this period a flock of newspapers, created to represent all shades of opinion, produced a fearful pell-mell of political principles. Blondet, the most judicious mind of the day, - judicious for others, never for himself, like some great lawyers unable to manage their own affairs, - was magnificent in such a discussion. The upshot was that he advised Nathan not to apostatize too suddenly.

"Napoleon said it; you can't make young republics of old monarchies. Therefore, my dear fellow, become the hero, the support, the creator of the Left Centre in the new Chamber, and you'll succeed. Once admitted into political ranks, once in the government, you can be what you like, - of any opinion that triumphs."

Nathan was bent on creating a daily political journal and becoming the absolute master of an enterprise which should absorb into it the countless little papers then swarming from the press, and establish ramifications with a review. He had seen so many fortunes made all around him by the press that he would not listen to Blondet, who warned him not to trust to such a venture, declaring that the plan was unsound, so great was the present number of newspapers, all fighting for subscribers. Raoul, relying on his so-called friends and his own courage, was all for daring it; he sprang up eagerly and said, with a proud gesture, -

"I shall succeed."

"But you haven't a sou."

Honore de Balzac

"I will write a play."

"It will fail."

"Let it fail!" replied Nathan.

He rushed through the various rooms of Florine's apartment, followed by Blondet, who thought him crazy, looking with a greedy eye upon the wealth displayed there. Blondet understood that look.

"There's a hundred and more thousand francs in them," he remarked.

"Yes," said Raoul, sighing, as he looked at Florine's sumptuous bedstead; "but I'd rather be a pedler all my life on the boulevard, and live on fried potatoes, than sell one item of this apartment."

"Not one item," said Blondet; "sell all. Ambition is like death; it takes all or nothing."

"No, a hundred times no! I would take anything from my new countess; but rob Florine of her shell? no."

"Upset our money-box, break one's balance-pole, smash our refuge, - yes, that would be serious," said Blondet with a tragic air.

"It seems to me from what I hear that you want to play politics instead of comedies," said Florine, suddenly appearing.

"Yes, my dear, yes," said Raoul, affectionately taking her by the neck and kissing her forehead. "Don't make faces at that; you won't lose anything. A minister can do better than a journalist for the queen of the boards. What parts and what holidays you shall have!"

"Where will you get the money?" she said.

"From my uncle," replied Raoul.

Florine knew Raoul's "uncle." The word meant usury, as in popular parlance "aunt" means pawn.

"Don't worry yourself, my little darling," said Blondet to Florine, tapping her shoulder. "I'll get him the assistance of Massol, a lawyer who wants to be deputy; also Finot, who has never yet got beyond his 'petit-journal,' and Pantin, who wants to be master of petitions, and who dabbles in reviews. Yes, I'll save him from himself; we'll convoke here to supper Etienne Lousteau, who can do the feuilleton; Claude Vignon for criticisms; Felicien Vernou as general care-taker; the lawyer will work, and du Tillet may take charge of the Bourse, the money article, and all industrial questions. We'll see where these various talents and slaves united will land the enterprise."

"In a hospital or a ministry, - where all men ruined in body or mind are apt to go," said Raoul, laughing.

"Where and when shall we invite them?"

"Here, five days hence."

"Tell me the sum you want," said Florine, simply.

"Well, the lawyer, du Tillet, and Raoul will each have to put up a hundred thousand francs before they embark on the affair," replied Blondet. "Then the paper can run eighteen months; about long enough for a rise and fall in Paris."

Florine gave a little grimace of approval. The two friends jumped into a cabriolet to go about collecting guests and pens, ideas and self-interests.

Florine meantime sent for certain dealers in old furniture, bric-a-brac, pictures, and jewels. These men entered her sanctuary and took an inventory of every article, precisely as if Florine were dead. She declared she would sell everything at public auction if they did not offer her a proper price. She had had the luck to please, she said, an English lord, and she wanted to get rid of all her property and look poor, so that he might give her a fine house and furniture, fit to rival the Rothschilds. But in spite of these persuasions and subterfuges, all the dealers would offer her for a mass of belongings worth a hundred and fifty thousand was seventy thousand. Florine thereupon offered to deliver over everything in eight days for eighty thousand, - "To take or leave," she said, - and the bargain was concluded. After the men had departed she skipped for joy, like the hills of King David, and performed all manner of follies, not having thought herself so rich.

When Raoul came back she made him a little scene, pretending to be hurt; she declared that he abandoned her; that she had reflected; men did not pass from one party to another, from the stage to the Chamber, without some reason; there was a woman at the bottom; she had a rival! In short, she made him swear eternal fidelity. Five days later she gave a splendid feast. The new journal was baptized in floods of wine and wit, with oaths of loyalty, fidelity, and good-fellowship. The name, forgotten now like those of the

Liberal, Communal, Departmental, Garde National, Federal, Impartial, was something in "al" that was equally imposing and evanescent. At three in the morning Florine could undress and go to bed as if alone, though no one had left the house; these lights of the epoch were sleeping the sleep of brutes. And when, early in the morning, the packers and vans arrived to remove Florine's treasures she laughed to see the porters moving the bodies of the celebrated men like pieces of furniture that lay in their way. "Sic transit" all her fine things! all her presents and souvenirs went to the shops of the various dealers, where no one on seeing them would know how those flowers of luxury had been originally paid for. It was agreed that a few little necessary articles should be left, for Florine's personal convenience until evening, - her bed, a table, a few chairs, and china enough to give her guests their breakfast.

Having gone to sleep beneath the draperies of wealth and luxury, these distinguished men awoke to find themselves within bare walls, full of nail-holes, degraded into abject poverty.

"Why, Florine! - The poor girl has been seized for debt!" cried Bixiou, who was one of the guests. "Quick! a subscription for her!"

On this they all roused up. Every pocket was emptied and produced a total of thirty-seven francs, which Raoul carried in jest to Florine's bedside. She burst out laughing and lifted her pillow, beneath which lay a mass of bank-notes to which she pointed.

Raoul called to Blondet.

"Ah! I see!" cried Blondet. "The little cheat has sold herself out without a word to us. Well done, you little angel!"

Thereupon, the actress was borne in triumph into the dining-room where most of the party still remained. The lawyer and du Tillet had departed.

That evening Florine had an ovation at the theatre; the story of her sacrifice had circulated among the audience.

"I'd rather be applauded for my talent," said her rival in the green-room.

"A natural desire in an actress who has never been applauded at all," remarked Florine.

During the evening Florine's maid installed her in Raoul's apartment in the Passage Sandrie. Raoul himself was to encamp in the house where the office of the new journal was established.

Such was the rival of the innocent Madame de Vandenesse. Raoul was the connecting link between the actress and the countess, - a knot severed by a duchess in the days of Louis XV. by the poisoning of Adrienne Lecouvreur; a not inconceivable vengeance, considering the offence.

Florine, however, was not in the way of Raoul's dawning passion. She foresaw the lack of money in the difficult enterprise he had undertaken, and she asked for leave of absence from the theatre. Raoul conducted the negotiation in a way to make himself more than ever valuable to her. With the good sense of the peasant in La Fontaine's fable, who makes sure of a dinner while the patricians talk, the actress went into the provinces to cut faggots for her celebrated man while he was employed in hunting power.

Honore de Balzac

CHAPTER VI

ROMANTIC LOVE

On the morrow of the ball given by Lady Dudley, Marie, without having received the slightest declaration, believed that she was loved by Raoul according to the programme of her dreams, and Raoul was aware that the countess had chosen him for her lover. Though neither had reached the incline of such emotions where preliminaries are abridged, both were on the road to it. Raoul, wearied with the dissipations of life, longed for an ideal world, while Marie, from whom the thought of wrong-doing was far, indeed, never imagined the possibility of going out of such a world. No love was ever more innocent or purer than theirs; but none was ever more enthusiastic or more entrancing in thought.

The countess was captivated by ideas worthy of the days of chivalry, though completely modernized. The glowing conversation of the poet had more echo in her mind than in her heart. She thought it fine to be his providence. How sweet the thought of supporting by her white and feeble hand this colossus, - whose feet of clay she did not choose to see; of giving life where life was needed; of being secretly the creator of a career; of helping a man of genius to struggle with fate and master it. Ah! to embroider his scarf for the tournament! To procure him weapons! to be his talisman against ill-fortune! his balm for every wound! For a woman brought up like Marie, religious and noble as she was, such a love was a form of charity. Hence the boldness of it. Pure sentiments often compromise them-selves with a lofty disdain that resembles the boldness of courtesans.

As soon as by her specious distinctions Marie had convinced herself that she did not in any way impair her conjugal faith, she rushed into the happiness of loving Raoul. The least little things of her daily life acquired a charm. Her boudoir, where she thought of him, became a sanctuary. There was nothing there that did not rouse some sense of pleasure; even her ink-stand was the coming accomplice in the pleasures of correspondence; for she would now have letters to read and answer. Dress, that splendid poesy of the feminine life, unknown or exhausted by her, appeared to her eyes endowed with a magic hitherto unperceived. It suddenly became clear to her what it is to most women, the manifestation of an inward thought, a language, a symbol. How many enjoyments in a toilet arranged to please *him*, to do *him* honor! She gave herself up ingenuously to all those gracefully charming things in which so many Parisian women spend their lives, and which give such significance to all that we see about them, and in them, and on them. Few women go to milliners and dressmakers for their own pleasure and interest. When old they never think of adornment. The next time you meet in the street a young woman stopping for a moment to look into a shop-window, examine her face carefully. "Will he think I look better in that?" are the words written on that fair brow, in the eyes sparkling with hope, in the smile that flickers on the lips.

Lady Dudley's ball took place on a Saturday night. On the following Monday the countess went to the Opera, feeling certain of seeing Raoul, who was, in fact, watching for her on one of the stairways leading down to the stalls. With what delight did she observe the unwonted care he had bestowed upon his clothes. This despiser of the laws of elegance had brushed and perfumed his hair; his waistcoat followed the fashion, his cravat was well tied, the bosom of his shirt was irreproachably smooth. Raoul was standing with his arms crossed as if posed for his portrait, magnificently indifferent to the rest of the audience and full of repressed impatience. Though lowered, his eyes were turned to the red velvet cushion on which lay Marie's arm. Felix, seated in the opposite corner of the box, had his back to Nathan.

So, in a moment, as it were, Marie had compelled this remarkable man to abjure his cynicism in the line of clothes. All women, high or low, are filled with delight on seeing a first proof of their power in one of these sudden metamorphoses. Such changes are an admission of serfdom.

"Those women were right; there is a great pleasure in being understood," she said to herself, thinking of her treacherous friends.

When the two lovers had gazed around the theatre with that glance that takes in everything, they exchanged a look of intelligence. It was for each as if some celestial dew had refreshed their hearts, burned-up with expectation.

"I have been here for an hour in purgatory, but now the heavens are opening," said Raoul's eyes.

"I knew you were waiting, but how could I help it?"
replied those of the countess.

Thieves, spies, lovers, diplomats, and slaves of any
kind alone know the resources and comforts of a
glance. They alone know what it contains of meaning,
sweetness, thought, anger, villainy, displayed by the
modification of that ray of light which conveys the
soul. Between the box of the Comtesse Felix de
Vandenesse and the step on which Raoul had perched
there were barely thirty feet; and yet it was impossible
to wipe out that distance. To a fiery being, who had
hitherto known no space between his wishes and their
gratification, this imaginary but insuperable gulf
inspired a mad desire to spring to the countess with the
bound of a tiger. In a species of rage he determined to
try the ground and bow openly to the countess. She
returned the bow with one of those slight inclinations
of the head with which women take from their adorers
all desire to continue their attempt. Comte Felix turned
round to see who had bowed to his wife; he saw
Nathan, but did not bow, and seemed to inquire the
meaning of such audacity; then he turned back slowly
and said a few words to his wife. Evidently the door of
that box was closed to Nathan, who cast a terrible look
of hatred upon Felix.

Madame d'Espard had seen the whole thing from her
box, which was just above where Raoul was standing.
She raised her voice in crying bravo to some singer,
which caused Nathan to look up to her; he bowed and
received in return a gracious smile which seemed to
say: -

"If they won't admit you there come here to me."

Raoul obeyed the silent summons and went to her box. He felt the need of showing himself in a place which might teach that little Vandenesse that fame was every whit as good as nobility, and that all doors turned on their hinges to admit him. The marquise made him sit in front of her. She wanted to question him.

"Madame Felix de Vandenesse is fascinating in that gown," she said, complimenting the dress as if it were a book he had published the day before.

"Yes," said Raoul, indifferently, "marabouts are very becoming to her; but she seems wedded to them; she wore them on Saturday," he added, in a careless tone, as if to repudiate the intimacy Madame d'Espard was fastening upon him.

"You know the proverb," she replied. "There is no good fete without a morrow."

In the matter of repartees literary celebrities are often not as quick as women. Raoul pretended dulness, a last resort for clever men.

"That proverb is true in my case," he said, looking gallantly at the marquise.

"My dear friend, your speech comes too late; I can't accept it," she said, laughing. "Don't be so prudish! Come, I know how it was; you complimented Madame de Vandenesse at the ball on her marabouts and she has put them on again for your sake. She likes you, and you adore her; it may be a little rapid, but it is all very natural. If I were mistaken you wouldn't be twisting your gloves like a man who is furious at having to sit here with me instead of flying to the box of his idol.

She has obtained," continued Madame d'Espard, glancing at his person impertinently, "certain sacrifices which you refused to make to society. She ought to be delighted with her success, - in fact, I have no doubt she is vain of it; I should be so in her place - immensely. She was never a woman of any mind, but she may now pass for one of genius. I am sure you will describe her in one of those delightful novels you write. And pray don't forget Vandenesse; put him in to please me. Really, his self-sufficiency is too much. I can't stand that Jupiter Olympian air of his, - the only mythological character exempt, they say, from ill-luck."

"Madame," cried Raoul, "you rate my soul very low if you think me capable of trafficking with my feelings, my affections. Rather than commit such literary baseness, I would do as they do in England, - put a rope round a woman's neck and sell her in the market."

"But I know Marie; she would like you to do it."

"She is incapable of liking it," said Raoul, vehemently.

"Oh! then you do know her well?"

Nathan laughed; he, the maker of scenes, to be trapped into playing one himself!

"Comedy is no longer there," he said, nodding at the stage; "it is here, in you."

He took his opera-glass and looked about the theatre to recover countenance.

"You are not angry with me, I hope?" said the

marquise, giving him a sidelong glance. "I should have had your secret somehow. Let us make peace. Come and see me; I receive every Wednesday, and I am sure the dear countess will never miss an evening if I let her know you will be there. So I shall be the gainer. Sometimes she comes between four and five o'clock, and I'll be kind and add you to the little set of favorites I admit at that hour."

"Ah!" cried Raoul, "how the world judges; it calls you unkind."

"So I am when I need to be," she replied. "We must defend ourselves. But your countess I adore; you will be contented with her; she is charming. Your name will be the first engraved upon her heart with that infantine joy that makes a lad cut the initials of his love on the barks of trees."

Raoul was aware of the danger of such conversations, in which a Parisian woman excels; he feared the marquise would extract some admission from him which she would instantly turn into ridicule among her friends. He therefore withdrew, prudently, as Lady Dudley entered.

"Well?" said the Englishwoman to the marquise, "how far have they got?"

"They are madly in love; he has just told me so."

"I wish he were uglier," said Lady Dudley, with a viperish look at Comte Felix. "In other respects he is just what I want him: the son of a Jew broker who died a bankrupt soon after his marriage; but the mother was a Catholic, and I am sorry to say she made a Christian of the boy."

This origin, which Nathan thought carefully concealed, Lady Dudley had just discovered, and she enjoyed by anticipation the pleasure she should have in launching some terrible epigram against Vandenesse.

"Heavens! I have just invited him to my house!" cried Madame d'Espard.

"Didn't I receive him at my ball?" replied Lady Dudley. "Some pleasures, my dear love, are costly."

The news of the mutual attachment between Raoul and Madame de Vandenesse circulated in the world after this, but not without exciting denials and incredulity. The countess, however, was defended by her friends, Lady Dudley, and Mesdames d'Espard and de Manerville, with an unnecessary warmth that gave a certain color to the calumny.

On the following Wednesday evening Raoul went to Madame d'Espard's, and was able to exchange a few sentences with Marie, more expressive by their tones than their ideas. In the midst of the elegant assembly both found pleasure in those enjoyable sensations given by the voice, the gestures, the attitude of one beloved. The soul then fastens upon absolute nothings. No longer do ideas or even language speak, but things; and these so loudly, that often a man lets another pay the small attentions - bring a cup of tea, or the sugar to sweeten it - demanded by the woman he loves, fearful of betraying his emotion to eyes that seem to see nothing and yet see all. Raoul, however, a man indifferent to the eyes of the world, betrayed his passion in his speech and was brilliantly witty. The company listened to the roar of a discourse inspired by the restraint put upon him; restraint being that which artists cannot endure. This Rolandic fury, this wit which slashed down all things, using epigram as its weapon, intoxicated Marie and amused the circle around them, as the sight of a bull goaded with banderols amuses the company in a Spanish circus.

"You may kick as you please, but you can't make a solitude about you," whispered Blondet.

The words brought Raoul to his senses, and he ceased to exhibit his irritation to the company. Madame d'Espard came up to offer him a cup of tea, and said loud enough for Madame de Vandenesse to hear: -

"You are certainly very amusing; come and see me sometimes at four o'clock."

The word "amusing" offended Raoul, though it was used as the ground of an invitation. Blondet took pity on him.

"My dear fellow," he said, taking him aside into a corner, you are behaving in society as if you were at Florine's. Here no one shows annoyance, or spouts long articles; they say a few words now and then, they look their calmest when most desirous of flinging others out of the window; they sneer softly, they pretend not to think of the woman they adore, and they are careful not to roll like a donkey on the high-road. In society, my good Raoul, conventions rule love. Either carry off Madame de Vandenesse, or show yourself a gentleman. As it is, you are playing the lover in one of your own books."

Nathan listened with his head lowered; he was like a lion caught in a toil.

"I'll never set foot in this house again," he cried. "That papier-mache marquise sells her tea too dear. She thinks me amusing! I understand now why Saint-Just wanted to guillotine this whole class of people."

"You'll be back here to-morrow."

Blondet was right. Passions are as mean as they are cruel. The next day after long hesitation between "I'll go - I'll not go," Raoul left his new partners in the midst of an important discussion and rushed to Madame d'Espard's house in the faubourg Saint-Honore. Beholding Rastignac's elegant cabriolet enter the court-yard while he was paying his cab at the gate, Nathan's vanity was stung; he resolved to have a cabriolet himself, and its accompanying tiger, too. The carriage of the countess was in the court-yard, and the sight of it swelled Raoul's heart with joy. Marie was advancing under the pressure of her desires with the regularity of the hands of a clock obeying the mainspring. He found her sitting at the corner of the fireplace in the little salon. Instead of looking at Nathan when he was announced, she looked at his reflection in a mirror.

"Monsieur le ministre," said Madame d'Espard, addressing Nathan, and presenting him to de Marsay by a glance, "was maintaining, when you came in, that the royalists and the republicans have a secret understanding. You ought to know something about it; is it so?"

"If it were so," said Raoul, "where's the harm? We hate

the same thing; we agree as to our hatreds, we differ only in our love. That's the whole of it."

"The alliance is odd enough," said de Marsay, giving a comprehensively meaning glance at the Comtesse Felix and Nathan.

"It won't last," said Rastignac, thinking, perhaps, wholly of politics.

"What do you think, my dear?" asked Madame d'Espard, addressing Marie.

"I know nothing of public affairs," replied the countess.

"But you soon will, madame," said de Marsay, "and then you will be doubly our enemy."

So saying he left the room with Rastignac, and Madame d'Espard accompanied them to the door of the first salon. The lovers had the room to themselves for a few moments. Marie held out her ungloved hand to Raoul, who took and kissed it as though he were eighteen years old. The eyes of the countess expressed so noble a tenderness that the tears which men of nervous temperament can always find at their service came into Raoul's eyes.

"Where can I see you? where can I speak with you?" he said. "It is death to be forced to disguise my voice, my look, my heart, my love -"

Moved by that tear Marie promised to drive daily in the Bois, unless the weather were extremely bad. This promise gave Raoul more pleasure than he had found in Florine for the last five years.

"I have so many things to say to you! I suffer from the silence to which we are condemned -"

The countess looked at him eagerly without replying, and at that moment Madame d'Espard returned to the room.

"Why didn't you answer de Marsay?" she said as she entered.

"We ought to respect the dead," replied Raoul. "Don't you see that he is dying? Rastignac is his nurse, - hoping to be put in the will."

The countess pretended to have other visits to pay, and left the house.

For this quarter of an hour Raoul had sacrificed important interests and most precious time. Marie was perfectly ignorant of the life of such men, involved in complicated affairs and burdened with exacting toil. Women of society are still under the influence of the traditions of the eighteenth century, in which all positions were definite and assured. Few women know the harassments in the life of most men who in these days have a position to make and to maintain, a fame to reach, a fortune to consolidate. Men of settled wealth and position can now be counted; old men alone have time to love; young men are rowing, like Nathan, the galleys of ambition. Women are not yet resigned to this change of customs; they suppose the same leisure of which they have too much in those who have none; they cannot imagine other occupations, other ends in life than their own. When a lover has vanquished the Lernean hydra in order to pay them a visit he has no merit in their eyes; they are only grateful to him for the pleasure he gives; they neither know nor care what it costs. Raoul became aware as he returned from this visit how difficult it would be to hold the reins of a love-affair in society, the ten-horsed chariot of journalism, his dramas on the stage, and his generally involved affairs.

"The paper will be wretched to-night," he thought, as he walked away. "No article of mine, and only the second number, too!"

Madame Felix de Vandenesse drove three times to the Bois de Boulogne without finding Raoul; the third time she came back anxious and uneasy. The fact was that Nathan did not choose to show himself in the Bois until he could go there as a prince of the press. He employed a whole week in searching for horses, a phantom and a suitable tiger, and in convincing his partners of the necessity of saving time so precious to them, and therefore of charging his equipage to the costs of the journal. His associates, Massol and du Tillet agreed to this so readily that he really believed them the best fellows in the world. Without this help, however, life would have been simply impossible to Raoul; as it was, it became so irksome that many men, even those of the strongest constitutions, could not have borne it. A violent and successful passion takes a great deal of space in an ordinary life; but when it is connected with a woman in the social position of Madame de Vandenesse it sucks the life out of a man as busy as Raoul. Here is a list of the obligations his passion imposed upon him.

Every day, or nearly every day, he was obliged to be

on horseback in the Bois, between two and three o'clock, in the careful dress of a gentleman of leisure. He had to learn at what house or theatre he could meet Madame de Vandenesse in the evening. He was not able to leave the party or the play until long after midnight, having obtained nothing better than a few tender sentences, long awaited, said in a doorway, or hastily as he put her into her carriage. It frequently happened that Marie, who by this time had launched him into the great world, procured for him invitations to dinner in certain houses where she went herself. All this seemed the simplest life in the world to her. Raoul moved by pride and led on by his passion never told her of his labors. He obeyed the will of this innocent sovereign, followed in her train, followed, also, the parliamentary debates, edited and wrote for his newspaper, and put upon the stage two plays, the money for which was absolutely indispensable to him. It sufficed for Madame de Vandenesse to make a little face of displeasure when he tried to excuse himself from attending a ball, a concert, or from driving in the Bois, to compel him to sacrifice his most pressing interests to her good pleasure. When he left society between one and two in the morning he went straight to work until eight or nine. He was scarcely asleep before he was obliged to be up and concocting the opinions of his journal with the men of political influence on whom he depended, - not to speak of the thousand and one other details of the paper. Journalism is connected with everything in these days; with industrial concerns, with public and private interests, with all new enterprises, and all the schemes of literature, its self-loves, and its products.

When Nathan, harassed and fatigued, would rush from his editorial office to the theatre, from the theatre to the

Chamber, from the Chamber to face certain creditors, he was forced to appear in the Bois with a calm countenance, and gallop beside Marie's carriage in the leisurely style of a man devoid of cares and with no other duties than those of love. When in return for this toilsome and wholly ignored devotion all he won were a few sweet words, the prettiest assurances of eternal attachment, ardent pressures of the hand on the very few occasions when they found themselves alone, he began to feel he was rather duped by leaving his mistress in ignorance of the enormous costs of these "little attentions," as our fathers called them. The occasion for an explanation arrived in due time.

On a fine April morning the countess accepted Nathan's arm for a walk through the sequestered path of the Bois de Boulogne. She intended to make him one of those pretty little quarrels apropos of nothing, which women are so fond of exciting. Instead of greeting him as usual, with a smile upon her lips, her forehead illumined with pleasure, her eyes bright with some gay or delicate thought, she assumed a grave and serious aspect.

"What is the matter?" said Nathan.

"Why do you pretend to such ignorance?" she replied. "You ought to know that a woman is not a child."

"Have I displeased you?"

"Should I be here if you had?"

"But you don't smile to me; you don't seem happy to see me."

"Oh! do you accuse me of sulking?" she said, looking at him with that submissive air which women assume when they want to seem victims.

Nathan walked on a few steps in a state of real apprehension which oppressed him.

"It must be," he said, after a moment's silence, "one of those frivolous fears, those hazy suspicions which women dwell on more than they do on the great things of life. You all have a way of tipping the world sideways with a straw, a cobweb -"

"Sarcasm!" she said, "I might have expected it!"

"Marie, my angel, I only said those words to wring your secret out of you."

"My secret would be always a secret, even if I told it to you."

"But all the same, tell it to me."

"I am not loved," she said, giving him one of those sly oblique glances with which women question so maliciously the men they are trying to torment.

"Not loved!" cried Nathan.

"No; you are too occupied with other things. What am I to you in the midst of them? forgotten on the least occasion! Yesterday I came to the Bois and you were not here -"

"But -"

"I had put on a new dress expressly to please you; you did not come; where were you?"

"But -"

"I did not know where. I went to Madame d'Espard's; you were not there."

"But -"

"That evening at the Opera, I watched the balcony; every time a door opened my heart was beating!"

"But -"

"What an evening I had! You don't reflect on such tempests of the heart."

"But -"

"Life is shortened by such emotions."

"But -"

"Well, what?" she said.

"You are right; life is shortened by them," said Nathan, "and in a few months you will utterly have consumed mine. Your unreasonable reproaches drag my secret from me - Ha! you say you are not loved; you are loved too well."

And thereupon he vividly depicted his position, told of his sleepless nights, his duties at certain hours, the absolute necessity of succeeding in his enterprise, the insatiable requirements of a newspaper in which he was required to judge the events of the whole world without blundering, under pain of losing his power, and so losing all, the infinite amount of rapid study he was forced to give to questions which passed as rapidly as clouds in this all-consuming age, etc., etc.

Raoul made a great mistake. The Marquise d'Espard had said to him on one occasion, "Nothing is more naive than a first love." As he unfolded before Marie's eyes this life which seemed to her immense, the countess was overcome with admiration. She had thought Nathan grand, she now considered him sublime. She blamed herself for loving him too much; begged him to come to her only when he could do so without difficulty. Wait? indeed she could wait! In future, she should know how to sacrifice her enjoyments. Wishing to be his stepping-stone was she really an obstacle? She wept with despair.

"Women," she said, with tears in her eyes, "can only love; men act; they have a thousand ways in which they are bound to act. But we can only think, and pray, and worship."

A love that had sacrificed so much for her sake deserved a recompense. She looked about her like a nightingale descending from a leafy covert to drink at a spring, to see if she were alone in the solitude, if the silence hid no witness; then she raised her head to Raoul, who bent his own, and let him take one kiss, the first and the only one that she ever gave in secret, feeling happier at that moment than she had felt in five years. Raoul thought all his toils well-paid. They both walked forward they scarcely knew where, but it was on the road to Auteuil; presently, however, they were forced to return and find their carriages, pacing together with the rhythmic step well-known to lovers. Raoul had faith in that kiss given with the quiet facility of a sacred sentiment. All the evil of it was in the mind of the world, not in that of the woman who walked beside him. Marie herself, given over to the grateful admiration which characterizes the love of woman, walked with a firm, light step on the gravelled path, saying, like Raoul, but few words; yet those few were felt and full of meaning. The sky was cloudless, the tall trees had burgeoned, a few green shoots were already brightening their myriad of brown twigs. The shrubs, the birches, the willows, the poplars were showing their first diaphanous and tender foliage. No soul resists these harmonies. Love explained Nature as it had already explained society to Marie's heart.

"I wish you have never loved any one but me," she said.

"Your wish is realized," replied Raoul. "We have awakened in each other the only true love."

He spoke the truth as he felt it. Posing before this innocent young heart as a pure man, Raoul was caught himself by his own fine sentiments. At first purely speculative and born of vanity, his love had now become sincere. He began by lying, he had ended in speaking truth. In all writers there is ever a sentiment, difficult to stifle, which impels them to admire the highest good. The countess, on her part, after her first rush of gratitude and surprise, was charmed to have inspired such sacrifices, to have caused him to surmount such difficulties. She was beloved by a man who was worthy of her! Raoul was totally ignorant to what his imaginary grandeur bound him. Women will not suffer their idol to step down from his pedestal.

They do not forgive the slightest pettiness in a god. Marie was far from knowing the solution to the riddle given by Raoul to his friends at Very's. The struggle of this writer, risen from the lower classes, had cost him the ten first years of his youth; and now in the days of his success he longed to be loved by one of the queens of the great world. Vanity, without which, as Champfort says, love would be but a feeble thing, sustained his passion and increased it day by day.

"Can you swear to me," said Marie, "that you belong and will never belong to any other woman?"

"There is neither time in my life nor place in my heart for any other woman," replied Raoul, not thinking that he told a lie, so little did he value Florine.

"I believe you," she said.

When they reached the alley where their carriages were waiting, Marie dropped Raoul's arm, and the young man assumed a respectful and distant attitude as if he had just met her; he accompanied her, with his hat off, to her carriage, then he followed her by the Avenue Charles X., breathing in, with satisfaction, the very dust her caleche raised.

In spite of Marie's high renunciations, Raoul continued to follow her everywhere; he adored the air of mingled pleasure and displeasure with which she scolded him for wasting his precious time. She took direction of his labors, she gave him formal orders on the employment of his time; she stayed at home to deprive him of every pretext for dissipation. Every morning she read his paper, and became the herald of his staff of editors, of Etienne Lousteau the feuilletonist, whom she thought delightful, of Felicien Vernou, of Claude Vignon, - in short, of the whole staff. She advised Raoul to do justice to de Marsay when he died, and she read with deep emotion the noble eulogy which Raoul published upon the dead minister while blaming his Machiavelianism and his hatred for the masses. She was present, of course, at the Gymnase on the occasion of the first representation of the play upon the proceeds of which Nathan relied to support his enterprise, and was completely duped by the purchased applause.

"You did not bid farewell to the Italian opera," said Lady Dudley, to whose house she went after the performance.

"No, I went to the Gymnase. They gave a first representation."

"I can't endure vaudevilles. I am like Louis XIV. about Teniers," said Lady Dudley.

"For my part," said Madame d'Espard, "I think actors have greatly improved. Vaudevilles in the present day are really charming comedies, full of wit, requiring great talent; they amuse me very much."

"The actors are excellent, too," said Marie. "Those at the Gymnase played very well to-night; the piece pleased them; the dialogue was witty and keen."

"Like those of Beaumarchais," said Lady Dudley.

"Monsieur Nathan is not Moliere as yet, but -" said Madame d'Espard, looking at the countess.

"He makes vaudevilles," said Madame Charles

de Vandenesse.

"And unmakes ministries," added Madame de Manerville.

The countess was silent; she wanted to answer with a sharp repartee; her heart was bounding with anger, but she could find nothing better to say than, -

"He will make them, perhaps."

All the women looked at each other with mysterious significance. When Marie de Vandenesse departed Moina de Saint-Heren exclaimed: -

"She adores him."

"And she makes no secret of it," said Madame d'Espard.

CHAPTER VII

SUICIDE

In the month of May Vandenesse took his wife, as usual, to their country-seat, where she was consoled by the passionate letters she received from Raoul, to whom she wrote every day.

Marie's absence might have saved Raoul from the gulf into which he was falling, if Florine had been near him; but, unfortunately, he was alone in the midst of friends who had become his enemies from the moment that he showed his intention of ruling them. His staff of writers hated him "pro tem.," ready to hold out a hand to him and console him in case of a fall, ready to adore him in case of success. So goes the world of literature. No one is really liked but an inferior. Every man's hand is against him who is likely to rise. This wide-spread envy doubles the chances of common minds who excite neither envy nor suspicion, who make their way like moles, and, fools though they be, find themselves gazetted in the "Moniteur," for three or four places, while men of talent are still struggling at t he doorto keep each other out.

The underhand enmity of these pretended friends, which Florine would have scented with the innate faculty of a courtesan to get at truth amid a thousand misleading circumstances, was by no means Raoul's greatest danger. His partners, Massol the lawyer, and du Tillet the banker, had intended from the first to harness his ardor to the chariot of their own importance and get rid of him as soon as he was out of condition to feed the paper, or else to deprive him of his power, arbitrarily, whenever it suited their purpose to take it. To them Nathan represented a certain amount of talent to use up, a literary force of the motive power of ten pens to employ. Massol, one of those lawyers who mistake the faculty of endless speech for eloquence, who possess the art of boring by diffusiveness, the torment of all meetings and assemblies where they belittle everything, and who desire to become personages at any cost, - Massol no longer wanted the place as Keeper of the Seals; he had seen some five or six different men go through that office in four years, and the robes disgusted him. In exchange, his mind was now set on obtaining a chair on the Board of Education and a place in the Council of State; the whole adorned with the cross of the Legion of honor. Du Tillet and Nucingen had guaranteed the cross to him, and the office of Master of Petitions provided he obeyed them blindly.

The better to deceive Raoul, these men allowed him to manage the paper without control. Du Tillet used it only for his stock-gambling, about which Nathan understood next to nothing; but he had given, through Nucingen, an assurance to Rastignac that the paper would be tacitly obliging to the government on the sole condition of supporting his candidacy for Monsieur de Nucingen's place as soon as he was nominated peer of France. Raoul was thus being undermined by the banker and the lawyer, who saw him with much satisfaction lording it in the newspaper, profiting by all advantages, and harvesting the fruits of self-love, while Nathan, enchanted, believed them to be, as on the occasion of his equestrian wants, the best fellows in the world. He thought he managed them! Men of imagination, to whom hope is the basis of existence, never allow themselves to know that the most perilous moment in their affairs is that when all seems going well according to their wishes.

This was a period of triumph by which Nathan profited. He appeared as a personage in the world, political and financial. Du Tillet presented him to the Nucingens. Madame de Nucingen received him cordially, less for himself than for Madame de Vandenesse; but when she ventured a few words about the countess he thought himself marvellously clever in using Florine as a shield; he alluded to his relations with the actress in a tone of generous self-conceit. How could he desert a great devotion, for the coquetries of the faubourg Saint-Germain?

Nathan, manipulated by Nucingen and Rastignac, by du Tillet and Blondet, gave his support ostentatiously to the "doctrinaires" of their new and ephemeral cabinet. But in order to show himself pure of all bribery he refused to take advantage of certain profitable enterprises which were started by means of his paper, - he! who had no reluctance in compromising friends or in behaving with little decency to mechanics under certain circumstances. Such meannesses, the result of vanity and of ambition, are found in many lives like his. The mantle must be splendid before the eyes of the world, and we steal our friend's or a poor man's cloth to patch it.

Nevertheless, two months after the departure of the

countess, Raoul had a certain Rabelaisian "quart d'heure" which caused him some anxiety in the midst of these triumphs. Du Tillet had advanced a hundred thousand francs, Florine's money had gone in the costs of the first establishment of the paper, which were enormous. It was necessary to provide for the future. The banker agreed to let the editor have fifty thousand francs on notes for four months. Du Tillet thus held Raoul by the halter of an IOU. By means of this relief the funds of the paper were secured for six months. In the eyes of some writers six months is an eternity. Besides, by dint of advertising and by offering illusory advantages to subscribers two thousand had been secured; an influx of travellers added to this semi-success, which was enough, perhaps, to excuse the throwing of more bank-bills after the rest. A little more display of talent, a timely political trial or crisis, an apparent persecution, and Raoul felt certain of becoming one of those modern "condottieri" whose ink is worth more than powder and shot of the olden time.

This loan from du Tillet was already made when Florine returned with fifty thousand francs. Instead of creating a savings fund with that sum, Raoul, certain of success (simply because he felt it was necessary), and already humiliated at having accepted the actress's money, deceived Florine as to his actual position, and persuaded her to employ the money in refurnishing her house. The actress, who did not need persuasion, not only spent the sum in hand, but she burdened herself with a debt of thirty thousand francs, with which she obtained a charming little house all to herself in the rue Pigale, whither her old society resorted. Raoul had reserved the production of his great piece, in which was a part especially suited to Florine, until her return. This comedy-vaudeville was to be Raoul's farewell to the stage. The newspapers, with that good nature which costs nothing, prepared the way for such an ovation to Florine that even the Theatre-Francais talked of engaging her. The feuilletons proclaimed her the heiress of Mars.

This triumph was sufficiently dazzling to prevent Florine from carefully studying the ground on which Nathan was advancing; she lived, for the time being, in a round of festivities and glory. According to those about her, he was now a great political character; he was justified in his enterprise; he would certainly be a deputy, probably a minister in course of time, like so many others. As for Nathan himself, he firmly believed that in the next session of the Chamber he should find himself in government with two other journalists, one of whom, already a minister, was anxious to associate some of his own craft with himself, and so consolidate his power. After a separation of six months, Nathan met Florine again with pleasure, and returned easily to his old way of life. All his comforts came from the actress, but he embroidered the heavy tissue of his life with the flowers of ideal passion; his letters to Marie were masterpieces of grace and style. Nathan made her the light of his life; he undertook nothing without consulting his "guardian angel." In despair at being on the popular side, he talked of going over to that of the aristocracy; but, in spite of his habitual agility, even he saw the absolute impossibility of such a jump; it was easier to become a minister. Marie's precious replies were deposited in one of those portfolios with patent locks made by Huret or Fichet, two mechanics who were then waging war in advertisements and posters all over Paris, as to which could make the safest and most impenetrable locks.

This portfolio was left about in Florine's new boudoir, where Nathan did much of his work. No one is easier to deceive than a woman to whom a man is in the habit of telling everything; she has no suspicions; she thinks she sees and hears and knows all. Besides, since her return, Nathan had led the most regular of lives under her very nose. Never did she imagine that that portfolio, which she hardly glanced at as it lay there unconcealed, contained the letters of a rival, treasures of admiring love which the countess addressed, at Raoul's request, to the office of his newspaper.

Nathan's situation was, therefore, to all appearance, extremely brilliant. He had many friends. The two plays lately produced had succeeded well, and their proceeds supplied his personal wants and relieved him of all care for the future. His debt to du Tillet, "his friend," did not make him in the least uneasy.

"Why distrust a friend?" he said to Blondet, who from time to time would cast a doubt on his position, led to do so by his general habit of analyzing.

"But we don't need to distrust our enemies," remarked Florine.

Nathan defended du Tillet; he was the best, the most upright of men.

This existence, which was really that of a dancer on the tight rope without his balance-pole, would have alarmed any one, even the most indifferent, had it been seen as it really was. Du Tillet watched it with the cool eye and the cynicism of a parvenu. Through the friendly good humor of his intercourse with Raoul there flashed now and then a malignant jeer. One day, after pressing his hand in Florine's boudoir and watching him as he got into his carriage, du Tillet remarked to Lousteau (envier par excellence): -

"That fellow is off to the Bois in fine style to-day, but he is just as likely, six months hence, to be in a debtor's prison."

"He? never!" cried Lousteau. "He has Florine."

"How do you know that he'll keep her? As for you, who are worth a dozen of him, I predict that you will be our editor-in-chief within six months."

In October Nathan's notes to du Tillet fell due, and the banker graciously renewed them, but for two months only, with the discount added and a fresh loan. Sure of victory, Raoul was not afraid of continuing to put his hand in the bag. Madame Felix de Vandenesse was to return in a few days, a month earlier than usual, brought back, of course, by her unconquerable desire to see Nathan, who felt that he could not be short of money at a time when he renewed that assiduous life.

Correspondence, in which the pen is always bolder than speech, and thought, wreathing itself with flowers, allows itself to be seen without disguise, and brought the countess to the highest pitch of enthusiasm. She believed she saw in Raoul one of the noblest spirits of the epoch, a delicate but misjudged heart without a stain and worthy of adoration; she saw him advancing with a brave hand to grasp the sceptre of power. Soon that speech so beautiful in love would echo from the tribune. Marie now lived only in this life of a world outside her own. Her taste was lost for the tranquil joys of home, and she gave herself up to the agitations of this whirlwind life communicated by a clever and adoring pen. She kissed Raoul's letters, written in the midst of the ceaseless battles of the press, with time taken from necessary studies; she felt their value; she was certain of being loved, and loved only, with no rival but the fame and ambition he adored. She found enough in her country solitude to fill her soul and employ her faculties, - happy, indeed, to have been so chosen by such a man, who to her was an angel.

During the last days of autumn Marie and Raoul again met and renewed their walks in the Bois, where alone they could see each other until the salons reopened. But when the winter fairly began, Raoul appeared in social life at his apogee. He was almost a personage. Rastignac, now out of power with the ministry, which went to pieces on the death of de Marsay, leaned upon Nathan, and gave him in return the warmest praise. Madame de Vandenesse, feeling this change in public opinion, was desirous of knowing if her husband's judgment had altered also. She questioned him again; perhaps with the hope of obtaining one of those brilliant revenges which please all women, even the noblest and least worldly, - for may we not believe that even the angels retain some portion of their self-love as they gather in serried ranks before the Holy of Holies?

"Nothing was wanting to Raoul Nathan but to be the dupe he now is to a parcel of intriguing sharpers," replied the count.

Felix, whose knowledge of the world and politics enabled him to judge clearly, had seen Nathan's true position. He explained to his wife that Fieschi's attempt had resulted in attaching to the interests threatened by this attack on Louis-Philippe a large body of hitherto lukewarm persons. The newspapers which were non-committal, and did not show their colors, would lose subscribers; for journalism, like politics, was about to be simplified by falling into regular lines. If Nathan had put his whole fortune into that newspaper he would lose it. This judgment, so apparently just and clear-cut, though brief and given by a man who fathomed a matter in which he had no interest, alarmed Madame de Vandenesse.

"Do you take an interest in him?" asked her husband.

"Only as a man whose mind interests me and whose conversation I like."

This reply was made so naturally that the count suspected nothing.

The next day at four o'clock, Marie and Raoul had a long conversation together, in a low voice, in Madame d'Espard's salon. The countess expressed fears which Raoul dissipated, only too happy to destroy by epigrams the conjugal judgment. Nathan had a revenge to take. He characterized the count as narrow-minded, behind the age, a man who judged the revolution of July with the eyes of the Restoration, who would never be willing to admit the triumph of the middle-classes - the new force of all societies, whether temporary or lasting, but a real force. Instead of turning his mind to the study of an opinion given impartially and incidentally by a man well-versed in politics, Raoul mounted his stilts and stalked about in the purple of his own glory. Where is the woman who would not have believed his glowing talk sooner than the cold logic of her husband? Madame de Vandenesse, completely reassured, returned to her life of little enjoyments, clandestine pressures of the hand, occasional quarrels, - in short, to her nourishment of the year before, harmless in itself, but likely to drag a woman over the border if the man she favors is resolute and impatient of obstacles. Happily for her, Nathan was not dangerous. Besides, he was too full of his immediate self-interests to think at this time of profiting by his love.

But toward the end of December, when the second notes fell due, du Tillet demanded payment. The rich banker, who said he was embarrassed, advised Raoul to borrow the money for a short time from a usurer, from Gigonnet, the providence of all young men who were pressed for money. In January, he remarked, the renewal of subscriptions to the paper would be coming in, there would be plenty of money in hand, and they could then see what had best be done. Besides, couldn't Nathan write a play? As a matter of pride Raoul determined to pay off the notes at once. Du Tillet gave Raoul a letter to Gigonnet, who counted out the money on a note of Nathan's at twenty days' sight. Instead of asking himself the reason of such unusual facility, Raoul felt vexed at his folly in not having asked for more. That is how men who are truly remarkable for the power of thought are apt to behave in practical business; they seem to reserve the power of their mind for their writings, and are fearful of lessening it by putting it to use in the daily affairs of life.

Raoul related his morning to Florine and Blondet. He gave them an inimitable sketch of Gigonnet, his fireplace without fire, his shabby wall-paper, his stairway, his asthmatic bell, his aged straw mattress, his den without warmth, like his eye. He made them laugh about this new uncle; they neither troubled themselves about du Tillet and his pretended want of money, nor about an old usurer so ready to disburse. What was there to worry about in that?

"He has only asked you fifteen per cent," said Blondet; "you ought to be grateful to him. At twenty-five per cent you don't bow to those old fellows. This is money-lending; usury doesn't begin till fifty per cent; and then you despise the usurer."

"Despise him!" cried Florine; "if any of your friends lent you money at that price they'd pose as your benefactors."

"She is right; and I am glad I don't owe anything now to du Tillet," said Raoul.

Why this lack of penetration as to their personal affairs in men whose business it is to penetrate all things? Perhaps the mind cannot be complete at all points; perhaps artists of every kind live too much in the present moment to study the future; perhaps they are too observant of the ridiculous to notice snares, or they may believe that none would dare to lay a snare for such as they. However this may be, the future arrived in due time. Twenty days later Raoul's notes were protested, but Florine obtained from the Court of commerce an extension of twenty-five days in which to meet them. Thus pressed, Raoul looked into his affairs and asked for the accounts, and it then appeared that the receipts of the newspaper covered only two-thirds of the expenses, while the subscriptions were rapidly dwindling. The great man now grew anxious and gloomy, but to Florine only, in whom he confided. She advised him to borrow money on unwritten plays, and write than at once, giving a lien on his work. Nathan followed this advice and obtained thereby twenty thousand francs, which reduced his debt to forty thousand.

On the 10th of February the twenty-five days expired. Du Tillet, who did not want Nathan as a rival before the electoral college, where he meant to appear himself, instigated Gigonnet to sue Nathan without compromise. A man locked up for debt could not present himself as a candidate for election. Florine was herself in communication with the sheriff on the subject of her personal debts, and no resource was left to her but the "I" of Medea, for her new furniture and belongings were now attached. The ambitious Raoul heard the cracking in all directions of his prosperous edifice, built, alas! without foundations. His nerve failed him; too weak already to sustain so vast an enterprise, he felt himself incapable of attempting to build it up again; he was fated to perish in its ashes. Love for the countess gave him still a few thrills of life; his mask brightened for a moment, but behind it hope was dead. He did not suspect the hand of du Tillet, and laid the blame of his misfortune on the usurer. Rastignac, Blondet, Lousteau, Vernou, Finot, and Massol took care not to enlighten him. Rastignac, who wanted to return to power, made common cause with Nucingen and du Tillet. The others felt a satisfaction in the catastrophe of an equal who had attempted to make himself their master. None of them, however, would have said a word to Florine; on the contrary, they praised Raoul to her.

"Nathan," they said, "has the shoulders of an Atlas; he'll pull himself through; all will come right."

"There were two new subscribers yesterday," said Blondet, gravely. "Raoul will certainly be elected deputy. As soon as the budget is voted the dissolution is sure to take place."

But Nathan, sued, could no longer obtain even usury; Florine, with all her personal property attached, could count on nothing but inspiring a passion in some fool who might not appear at the right moment. Nathan's friends were all men without money and without credit. An arrest for debt would destroy his hopes of a political career; and besides all this, he had bound himself to do an immense amount of dramatic work for which he had already received payment. He could see no bottom to the gulf of misery that lay before him, into which he was about to roll. In presence of such threatened evil his boldness deserted him. Would the Comtesse de Vandenesse stand by him? Would she fly with him? Women are never led into a gulf of that kind except by an absolute love, and the love of Raoul and Marie had not bound them together by the mysterious and inalienable ties of happiness. But supposing that the countess did follow him to some foreign country; she would come without fortune, despoiled of everything, and then, alas! she would merely be one more embarrassment to him. A mind of a second order, and a proud mind like that of Nathan, would be likely to see, under these circumstances, and did see, in suicide the sword to cut the Gordian knots. The idea of failure in the face of the world and that society he had so lately entered and meant to rule, of leaving the chariot of the countess and becoming once more a muddied pedestrian, was more than he could bear. Madness began to dance and whirl and shake her bells at the gates of the fantastic palace in which the poet had been dreaming. In this extremity, Nathan waited for some lucky accident, determined not to kill himself until the final moment.

During the last days employed by the legal formalities required before proceeding to arrest for debt, Raoul went about, in spite of himself, with that coldly sullen and morose expression of face which may be noticed in persons who are either fated to commit suicide or are meditating it. The funereal ideas they are turning over in their minds appear upon their foreheads in gray and cloudy tints, their smile has something fatalistic in it, their motions are solemn. These unhappy beings seem to want to suck the last juices of the life they mean to leave; their eyes see things invisible, their ears are listening to a death-knell, they pay no attention to the minor things about them. These alarming symptoms Marie perceived one evening at Lady Dudley's. Raoul was sitting apart on a sofa in the boudoir, while the rest of the company were conversing in the salon. The countess went to the door, but he did not raise his head; he heard neither Marie's breathing nor the rustle of her silk dress; he was gazing at a flower in the carpet, with fixed eyes, stupid with grief; he felt he had rather die than abdicate. All the world can't have the rock of Saint Helena for a pedestal. Moreover, suicide was then the fashion in Paris. Is it not, in fact, the last resource of all atheistical societies? Raoul, as he sat there, had decided that the moment had come to die. Despair is in proportion to our hopes; that of Raoul had no other issue than the grave.

"What is the matter?" cried Marie, flying to him.

"Nothing," he answered.

There is one way of saying that word "nothing"

between lovers which signifies its exact contrary. Marie shrugged her shoulders.

"You are a child," she said. "Some misfortune has happened to you."

"No, not to me," he replied. "But you will know all soon enough, Marie," he added, affectionately.

"What were you thinking of when I came in?" she asked, in a tone of authority.

"Do you want to know the truth?" She nodded. "I was thinking of you; I was saying to myself that most men in my place would have wanted to be loved without reserve. I am loved, am I not?"

"Yes," she answered.

"And yet," he said, taking her round the waist and kissing her forehead at the risk of being seen, "I leave you pure and without remorse. I could have dragged you into an abyss, but you remain in all your glory on its brink without a stain. Yet one thought troubles me -"

"What is it?" she asked.

"You will despise me." She smiled superbly. "Yes, you will never believe that I have sacredly loved you; I shall be disgraced, I know that. Women never imagine that from the depths of our mire we raise our eyes to heaven and truly adore a Marie. They assail that sacred love with miserable doubts; they cannot believe that men of intellect and poesy can so detach their soul from earthly enjoyment as to lay it pure upon some cherished altar. And yet, Marie, the worship of the ideal is more fervent in men then in women; we find it in women, who do not even look for it in us."

"Why are you making me that article?" she said, jestingly.

"I am leaving France; and you will hear to-morrow, how and why, from a letter my valet will bring you. Adieu, Marie."

Raoul left the house after again straining the countess to his heart with dreadful pressure, leaving her stupefied and distressed.

"What is the matter, my dear?" said Madame d'Espard, coming to look for her. "What has Monsieur Nathan been saying to you? He has just left us in a most melodramatic way. Perhaps you are too reasonable or too unreasonable with him."

The countess got into a hackney-coach and was driven rapidly to the newspaper office. At that hour the huge apartments which they occupied in an old mansion in the rue Feydeau were deserted; not a soul was there but the watchman, who was greatly surprised to see a young and pretty woman hurrying through the rooms in evident distress. She asked him to tell her where was Monsieur Nathan.

"At Mademoiselle Florine's, probably," replied the man, taking Marie for a rival who intended to make a scene.

"Where does he work?"

"In his office, the key of which he carries in his pocket."

"I wish to go there."

The man took her to a dark little room looking out on a rear court-yard. The office was at right angles. Opening the window of the room she was in, the countess could look through into the window of the office, and she saw Nathan sitting there in the editorial arm-chair.

"Break in the door, and be silent about all this; I'll pay you well," she said. "Don't you see that Monsieur Nathan is dying?"

The man got an iron bar from the press-room, with which he burst in the door. Raoul had actually smothered himself, like any poor work-girl, with a pan of charcoal. He had written a letter to Blondet, which lay on the table, in which he asked him to ascribe his death to apoplexy. The countess, however, had arrived in time; she had Raoul carried to her coach, and then, not knowing where else to care for him, she took him to a hotel, engaged a room, and sent for a doctor. In a few hours Raoul was out of danger; but the countess did not leave him until she had obtained a general confession of the causes of his act. When he had poured into her heart the dreadful elegy of his woes, she said, in order to make him willing to live: -

"I can arrange all that."

But, nevertheless, she returned home with a heart oppressed with the same anxieties and ideas that had darkened Nathan's brow the night before.

"Well, what was the matter with your sister?" said Felix, when his wife returned. "You look distressed."

"It is a dreadful history about which I am bound to secrecy," she said, summoning all her nerve to appear calm before him.

In order to be alone and to think at her ease, she went to the Opera in the evening, after which she resolved to go (as we have seen) and discharge her heart into that of her sister, Madame du Tillet; relating to her the horrible scene of the morning, and begging her advice and assistance. Neither the one nor the other could then know that du Tillet himself had lighted the charcoal of the vulgar brazier, the sight of which had so justly terrified the countess.

"He has but me in all the world," said Marie to her sister, "and I will not fail him."

That speech contains the secret motive of most women; they can be heroic when they are certain of being all in all to a grand and irreproachable being.

CHAPTER VIII

A LOVER SAVED AND LOST

Du Tillet had heard some talk even in financial circles of the more or less possible adoration of his sister-in-law for Nathan; but he was one of those who denied it, thinking it incompatible with Raoul's known relations with Florine. The actress would certainly drive off the countess, or vice versa. But when, on coming home that evening, he found his sister-in-law with a perturbed face, in consultation with his wife about money, it occurred to him that Raoul had, in all probability, confided to her his situation. The countess must therefore love him; she had doubtless come to obtain from her sister the sum due to old Gigonnet. Madame du Tillet, unaware, of course, of the reasons for her husband's apparently supernatural penetration, had shown such stupefaction when he told her the sum wanted, that du Tillet's suspicions became certainties. He was sure now that he held the thread of all Nathan's possible manoeuvres.

No one knew that the unhappy man himself was in bed in a small hotel in the rue du Mail, under the name of the office watchman, to whom Marie had promised five hundred francs if he kept silence as to the events of the preceding night and morning. Thus bribed, the man, whose name was Francois Quillet, went back to the office and left word with the portress that Monsieur Nathan had been taken ill in consequence of overwork, and was resting. Du Tillet was therefore not surprised at Raoul's absence. It was natural for the journalist to hide under any such pretence to avoid arrest. When the sheriff's spies made inquiries they learned that a lady had carried him away in a public coach early in the morning; but it took three days to ferret out the number of the coach, question the driver, and find the hotel where the debtor was recovering his strength. Thus Marie's prompt action had really gained for Nathan a truce of four days.

Both sisters passed a cruel night. Such a catastrophe casts the lurid gleams of its charcoal over the whole of life, showing reefs, pools, depths, where the eye has hitherto seen only summits and grandeurs. Struck by the horrible picture of a young man lying back in his chair to die, with the last proofs of his paper before him, containing in type his last thoughts, poor Madame du Tillet could think of nothing else than how to save him and restore a life so precious to her sister. It is the nature of our mind to see effects before we analyze their causes. Eugenie recurred to her first idea of consulting Madame Delphine de Nucingen, with whom she was to dine, and she resolved to make the attempt, not doubting of success. Generous, like all persons who are not bound in the polished steel armor of modern society, Madame du Tillet resolved to take the whole matter upon herself.

The countess, on the other hand, happy in the thought that she had saved Raoul's life, spent the night in devising means to obtain the forty thousand francs. In emergencies like these women are sublime; they find contrivances which would astonish thieves, business

Honore de Balzac

men, and usurers, if those three classes of industrials were capable of being astonished. First, the countess sold her diamonds and decided on wearing paste; then she resolved to ask the money from Vandenesse on her sister's account; but these were dishonorable means, and her soul was too noble not to recoil at them; she merely conceived them, and cast them from her. Ask money of Vandenesse to give to Nathan! She bounded in her bed with horror at such baseness. Wear false diamonds to deceive her husband! Next she thought of borrowing the money from the Rothschilds, who had so much, or from the archbishop of Paris, whose mission it was to help persons in distress; darting thus from thought to thought, seeking help in all. She deplored belonging to a class opposed to the government. Formerly, she could easily have borrowed the money on the steps of the throne. She thought of appealing to her father, the Comte de Granville. But that great magistrate had a horror of illegalities; his children knew how little he sympathized with the trials of love; he was now a misanthrope and held all affairs of the heart in horror. As for the Comtesse de Granville, she was living a retired life on one of her estates in Normandy, economizing and praying, ending her days between priests and money-bags, cold as ever to her dying moment. Even supposing that Marie had time to go to Bayeux and implore her, would her mother give her such a sum unless she explained why she wanted it? Could she say she had debts? Yes, perhaps her mother would be softened by the wants of her favorite child. Well, then! in case all other means failed, she *would* go to Normandy. The dreadful sight of the morning, the effects she had made to revive Nathan, the hours passed beside his pillow, his broken confession, the agony of a great soul, a vast genius stopped in its upward flight by a sordid vulgar obstacle, - all these things rushed into her memory and stimulated her love. She went over and over her emotions, and felt her love to be deeper in these days of misery than in those of Nathan's fame and grandeur. She felt the nobility of his last words said to her in Lady Dudley's boudoir. What sacredness in that farewell! What grandeur in the immolation of a selfish happiness which would have been her torture! The countess had longed for emotions, and now she had them, - terrible, cruel, and yet most precious. She lived a deeper life in pain than in pleasure. With what delight she said to herself: "I have saved him once, and I will save him again." She heard him cry out when he felt her lips upon his forehead, "Many a poor wretch does not know what love is!"

"Are you ill?" said her husband, coming into her room to take her to breakfast.

"I am dreadfully worried about a matter that is happening at my sister's," she replied, without actually telling a lie.

"Your sister has fallen into bad hands," replied Felix. "It is a shame for any family to have a du Tillet in it, - a man without honor of any kind. If disaster happened to her she would get no pity from him."

"What woman wants pity?" said the countess, with a convulsive motion. "A man's sternness is to us our only pardon."

"This is not the first time that I read your noble heart," said the count. "A woman who thinks as you do needs no watching."

Honore de Balzac

"Watching!" she said; "another shame that recoils on you."

Felix smiled, but Marie blushed. When women are secretly to blame they often show ostensibly the utmost womanly pride. It is a dissimulation of mind for which we ought to be obliged to them. The deception is full of dignity, if not of grandeur. Marie wrote two lines to Nathan under the name of Monsieur Quillet, to tell him that all went well, and sent them by a street porter to the hotel du Mail. That night, at the Opera, Felix thought it very natural that she should wish to leave her box and go to that of her sister, and he waited till du Tillet had left his wife to give Marie his arm and take her there. Who can tell what emotions agitated her as she went through the corridors and entered her sister's box with a face that was outwardly serene and calm!

"Well?" she said, as soon as they were alone.

Eugenie's face was an answer; it was bright with a joy which some persons might have attributed to the satisfaction of vanity.

"He can be saved, dear; but for three months only; during which time we must plan some other means of doing it permanently. Madame de Nucingen wants four notes of hand, each for ten thousand francs, endorsed by any one, no matter who, so as not to compromise you. She explained to me how they were made, but I couldn't understand her. Monsieur Nathan, however, can make them for us. I thought of Schmucke, our old master. I am sure he could be very useful in this emergency; he will endorse the notes. You must add to the four notes a letter in which you guarantee their payment to Madame de Nucingen, and she will give you the money to-morrow. Do the whole thing yourself; don't trust it to any one. I feel sure that Schmucke will make no objection. To divert all suspicion I told Madame de Nucingen you wanted to oblige our old music-master who was in distress, and I asked her to keep the matter secret."

"You have the sense of angels! I only hope Madame de Nucingen won't tell of it until after she gives me the money," said the countess.

"Schmucke lives in the rue de Nevers on the quai Conti; don't forget the address, and go yourself."

"Thanks!" said the countess, pressing her sister's hand. "Ah! I'd give ten years of life -"

"Out of your old age -"

"If I could put an end to these anxieties," said the countess, smiling at the interruption.

The persons who were at that moment levelling their opera-glasses at the two sisters might well have supposed them engaged in some light-hearted talk; but any observer who had come to the Opera more for the pleasure of watching faces than for mere idle amusement might have guessed them in trouble, from the anxious look which followed the momentary smiles on their charming faces. Raoul, who did not fear the bailiffs at night, appeared, pale and ashy, with anxious eye and gloomy brow, on the step of the staircase where he regularly took his stand. He looked for the Countess in her box and, finding it empty, buried his face in his hands, leaning his elbows on the balustrade.

"Can she be here!" he thought.

"Look up, unhappy hero," whispered Mme. du Tillet.

As for Marie, at all risks she fixed on him that steady magnetic gaze, in which the will flashes from the eye, as rays of light from the sun. Such a look, mesmerizers say, penetrates to the person on whom it is directed, and certainly Raoul seemed as though struck by a magic wand. Raising his head, his eyes met those of the sisters. With that charming feminine readiness which is never at fault, Mme. De Vandenesse seized a cross, sparkling on her neck, and directed his attention to it by a swift smile, full of meaning. The brilliance of the gem radiated even upon Raoul's forehead, and he replied with a look of joy; he had understood.

"Is it nothing then, Eugenie," said the Countess, "thus to restore life to the dead?"

"You have a chance yet with the Royal Humane Society," replied Eugenie, with a smile."

"How wretched and depressed he looked when he came, and how happy he will go away!"

At this moment du Tillet, coming up to Raoul with every mark of friendliness, pressed his hand, and said:

"Well, old fellow, how are you?"

"As well as a man is likely to be who has just got the best possible news of the election. I shall be successful," replied Raoul, radiant.

"Delighted," said du Tillet. "We shall want money for

the paper."

"The money will be found," said Raoul.

"The devil is with these women!" exclaimed du Tillet, still unconvinced by the words of Raoul, whom he had nicknamed Charnathan.

"What are you talking about?" said Raoul.

"My sister-in-law is there with my wife, and they are hatching something together. You seem in high favor with the Countess; she is bowing to you right across the house."

"Look," said Mme. du Tillet to her sister, "they told us wrong. See how my husband fawns on M. Nathan, and it is he who they declared was trying to get him put in prison!"

"And men call us slanderers!" cried the Countess. "I will give him a warning."

She rose, took the arm of Vandenesse, who was waiting in the passage, and returned jubilant to her box; by and by she left the Opera and ordered her carriage for the next morning before eight o'clock.

The next morning, by half-past eight, Marie had driven to the quai Conti, stopping at the hotel du Mail on her way. The carriage could not enter the narrow rue de Nevers; but as Schmucke lived in a house at the corner of the quai she was not obliged to walk up its muddy pavement, but could jump from the step of her carriage to the broken step of the dismal old house, mended like porter's crockery, with iron rivets, and bulging out over the street in a way that was quite alarming to pedestrians. The old chapel-master lived on the fourth floor, and enjoyed a fine view of the Seine from the pont Neuf to the heights of Chaillot.

The good soul was so surprised when the countess's footman announced the visit of his former scholar that in his stupefaction he let her enter without going down to receive her. Never did the countess suspect or imagine such an existence as that which suddenly revealed itself to her eyes, though she had long known Schmucke's contempt for dress, and the little interest he held in the affairs of this world. But who could have believed in such complete indifference, in the utter laisser-aller of such a life? Schmucke was a musical Diogenes, and he felt no shame whatever in his untidiness; in fact, he was so accustomed to it that he would probably have denied its existence. The incessant smoking of a stout German pipe had spread upon the ceiling and over a wretched wall-paper, scratched and defaced by the cat, a yellowish tinge. The cat, a magnificently long-furred, fluffy animal, the envy of all portresses, presided there like the mistress of the house, grave and sedate, and without anxieties. On the top of an excellent Viennese piano he sat majestically, and cast upon the countess, as she entered, that coldly gracious look which a woman, surprised by the beauty of another woman, might have given. He did not move, and merely waved the two silver threads of his right whisker as he turned his golden eyes on Schmucke.

The piano, decrepit on its legs, though made of good wood painted black and gilded, was dirty, defaced, and scratched; and its keys, worn like the teeth of old horses, were yellowed with the fuliginous colors of the pipe. On the desk, a little heap of ashes showed that the night before Schmucke had bestrode the old instrument to some musical Walhalla. The floor, covered with dried mud, torn papers, tobacco-dust, fragments indescribable, was like that of a boy's school-room, unswept for a week, on which a mound of things accumulate, half rags, half filth.

A more practised eye than that of the countess would have seen certain other revelations of Schmucke's mode of life, - chestnut-peels, apple-parings, egg-shells dyed red in broken dishes smeared with sauer-kraut. This German detritus formed a carpet of dusty filth which crackled under foot, joining company near the hearth with a mass of cinders and ashes descending majestically from the fireplace, where lay a block of coal, before which two slender twigs made a show of burning. On the chimney-piece was a mirror in a painted frame, adorned with figures dancing a saraband; on one side hung the glorious pipe, on the other was a Chinese jar in which the musician kept his tobacco. Two arm-chairs bought at auction, a thin and rickety cot, a worm-eaten bureau without a top, a maimed table on which lay the remains of a frugal breakfast, made up a set of household belongings as plain as those of an Indian wigwam. A shaving-glass, suspended to the fastening of a curtainless window, and surmounted by a rag striped by many wipings of a razor, indicated the only sacrifices paid by Schmucke to the Graces and society. The cat, being the feebler and protected partner, had rather the best of the establishment; he enjoyed the comforts of an old sofa-cushion, near which could be seen a white china cup and plate. But what no pen can describe was the state into which Schmucke, the cat, and the pipe, that existing trinity, had reduced these articles. The pipe had burned the table. The cat and Schmucke's head had greased the green Utrecht velvet of the two arm-chairs and reduced it to a slimy texture. If it had not been for the cat's magnificent tail, which played a useful part in the household, the uncovered places on the bureau and the piano would never have been dusted. In one corner of the room were a pile of shoes which need an epic to describe them. The top of the bureau and that of the piano were encumbered by music-books with ragged backs and whitened corners, through which the pasteboard showed its many layers. Along the walls the names and addresses of pupils written on scraps of paper were stuck on by wafers, - the number of wafers without paper indicating the number of pupils no longer taught. On the wall-papers were many calculations written with chalk. The bureau was decorated with beer-mugs used the night before, their newness appearing very brilliant in the midst of this rubbish of dirt and age. Hygiene was represented by a jug of water with a towel laid upon it, and a bit of common soap. Two ancient hats hung to their respective nails, near which also hung the self-same blue box-coat with three capes, in which the countess had always seen Schmucke when he came to give his lessons. On the window-sill were three pots of flowers, German flowers, no doubt, and near them a stout hollywood stick.

Though Marie's sight and smell were disagreeably affected, Schmucke's smile and glance disguised these abject miseries by rays of celestial light which actually illuminated their smoky tones and vivified the chaos. The soul of this dear man, which saw and revealed so many things divine, shone like the sun. His laugh, so frank, so guileless at seeing one of his Saint-Cecilias, shed sparkles of youth and gaiety and innocence about him. The treasures he poured from the inner to the outer were like a mantle with which he covered his squalid life. The most supercilious parvenu would have felt it ignoble to care for the frame in which this glorious old apostle of the musical religion lived and moved and had his being.

"Hey! by what good luck do I see you here, dear Madame la comtesse?" he said. "Must I sing the canticle of Simeon at my age?" (This idea so tickled him that he laughed immoderately.) "Truly I'm 'en bonne fortune.'" (And again he laughed like a merry child.) "But, ah!" he said, changing to melancholy, "you come for the music, and not for a poor old man like me. Yes, I know that; but come for what you will, I am yours, you know, body and soul and all I have!"

This was said in his unspeakable German accent, a rendition of which we spare the reader.

He took the countess's hand, kissed it and left a tear there, for the worthy soul was always on the morrow of her benefit. Then he seized a bit of chalk, jumped on a chair in front of the piano, and wrote upon the wall in big letters, with the rapidity of a young man, "February 17th, 1835." This pretty, artless action, done in such a passion of gratitude, touched the countess to tears.

"My sister will come too," she said.

"The other, too! When? when? God grant it be before I die!"

"She will come to thank you for a great service I am now here to ask of you."

"Quick! quick! tell me what it is," cried Schmucke. "What must I do? go to the devil?"

"Nothing more than write the words 'Accepted for ten thousand francs,' and sign your name on each of these papers," she said, taking from her muff four notes prepared for her by Nathan.

"Hey! that's soon done," replied the German, with the docility of a lamb; "only I'm sure I don't know where my pens and ink are - Get away from there, Meinherr Mirr!" he cried to the cat, which looked composedly at him. "That's my cat," he said, showing him to the countess. "That's the poor animal that lives with poor Schmucke. Hasn't he fine fur?"

"Yes," said the countess.

"Will you have him?" he cried.

"How can you think of such a thing?" she answered. "Why, he's your friend!"

The cat, who hid the inkstand behind him, divined that Schmucke wanted it, and jumped to the bed.

"He's as mischievous as a monkey," said Schmucke. "I call him Mirr in honor of our great Hoffman of Berlin, whom I knew well."

The good man signed the papers with the innocence of a child who does what his mother orders without question, so sure is he that all is right. He was thinking much more of presenting the cat to the countess than of the papers by which his liberty might be, according to the laws relating to foreigners, forever sacrificed.

"You assure me that these little papers with the stamps on them -"

"Don't be in the least uneasy," said the countess.

"I am not uneasy," he said, hastily. "I only meant to ask if these little papers will give pleasure to Madame du Tillet."

"Oh, yes," she said, "you are doing her a service, as if you were her father."

"I am happy, indeed, to be of any good to her - Come and listen to my music!" and leaving the papers on the table, he jumped to his piano.

The hands of this angel ran along the yellowing keys, his glance was rising to heaven, regardless of the roof; already the air of some blessed climate permeated the room and the soul of the old musician; but the countess did not allow the artless interpreter of things celestial to make the strings and the worn wood speak, like Raffaelle's Saint Cecilia, to the listening angels. She quickly slipped the notes into her muff and recalled her radiant master from the ethereal spheres to which he soared, by laying her hand upon his shoulder.

"My good Schmucke -" she said.

"Going already?" he cried. "Ah! why did you come?"

He did not murmur, but he sat up like a faithful dog who listens to his mistress.

"My good Schmucke," she repeated, "this is a matter of life and death; minutes can save tears, perhaps blood."

"Always the same!" he said. "Go, angel! dry the tears of others. Your poor Schmucke thinks more of your visit than of your gifts."

"But we must see each other often," she said. "You must come and dine and play to me every Sunday, or we shall quarrel. Remember, I shall expect you next Sunday."

"Really and truly?"

"Yes, I entreat you; and my sister will want you, too, for another day."

"Then my happiness will be complete," he said; "for I only see you now in the Champs Elysees as you pass in your carriage, and that is very seldom."

This thought dried the tears in his eyes as he gave his arm to his beautiful pupil, who felt the old man's heart beat violently.

"You think of us?" she said.

"Always as I eat my food," he answered, - "as my benefactresses; but chiefly as the first young girls worthy of love whom I ever knew."

So respectful, faithful, and religious a solemnity was in this speech that the countess dared say no more. That smoky chamber, full of dirt and rubbish, was the temple of the two divinities.

"There we are loved - and truly loved," she thought.

The emotion with which old Schmucke saw the

countess get into her carriage and leave him she fully shared, and she sent him from the tips of her fingers one of those pretty kisses which women give each other from afar. Receiving it, the old man stood planted on his feet for a long time after the carriage had disappeared.

A few moments later the countess entered the courtyard of the hotel de Nucingen. Madame de Nucingen was not yet up; but anxious not to keep a woman of the countess's position waiting, she hastily threw on a shawl and wrapper.

"My visit concerns a charitable action, madame," said the countess, "or I would not disturb you at so early an hour."

"But I am only too happy to be disturbed," said the banker's wife, taking the notes and the countess's guarantee. She rang for her maid.

"Therese," she said, "tell the cashier to bring me up himself, immediately, forty thousand francs."

Then she locked into a table drawer the guarantee given by Madame de Vandenesse, after sealing it up.

"You have a delightful room," said the countess.

"Yes, but Monsieur de Nucingen is going to take it from me. He is building a new house."

"You will doubtless give this one to your daughter, who, I am told, is to marry Monsieur de Rastignac."

The cashier appeared at this moment with the money.

Madame de Nucingen took the bank-bills and gave him the notes of hand.

"That balances," she said.

"Except the discount," replied the cashier. "Ha, Schmucke; that's the musician of Anspach," he added, examining the signatures in a suspicious manner that made the countess tremble.

"Who is doing this business?" said Madame de Nucingen, with a haughty glance at the cashier. "This is my affair."

The cashier looked alternately at the two ladies, but he could discover nothing on their impenetrable faces.

"Go, leave us - Have the kindness to wait a few moments that the people in the bank may not connect you with this negotiation," said Madame de Nucingen to the countess.

"I must ask you to add to all your other kindness that of keeping this matter secret," said Madame de Vandenesse.

"Most assuredly, since it is for charity," replied the baroness, smiling. "I will send your carriage round to the garden gate, so that no one will see you leave the house."

"You have the thoughtful grace of a person who has suffered," said the countess.

"I do not know if I have grace," said the baroness; "but I have suffered much. I hope that your anxieties cost less than mine."

When a man has laid a plot like that du Tillet was scheming against Nathan, he confides it to no man. Nucingen knew something of it, but his wife knew nothing. The baroness, however, aware that Raoul was embarrassed, was not the dupe of the two sisters; she guessed into whose hands that money was to go, and she was delighted to oblige the countess; moreover, she felt a deep compassion for all such embarrassments. Rastignac, so placed that he was able to fathom the manoeuvres of the two bankers, came to breakfast that morning with Madame de Nucingen.

Delphine and Rastignac had no secrets from each other; and the baroness related to him her scene with the countess. Eugene, who had never supposed that Delphine could be mixed up in the affair, which was only accessory to his eyes, - one means among many others, - opened her eyes to the truth. She had probably, he told her, destroyed du Tillet's chances of selection, and rendered useless the intrigues and deceptions of the past year. In short, he put her in the secret of the whole affair, advising her to keep absolute silence as to the mistake she had just committed.

"Provided the cashier does not tell Nucingen," she said.

A few moments after mid-day, while du Tillet was breakfasting, Monsieur Gigonnet was announced.

"Let him come in," said the banker, though his wife was at table. "Well, my old Shylock, is our man locked up?"

"No."

"Why not? Didn't I give you the address, rue du Mail, hotel -"

"He has paid up," said Gigonnet, drawing from his wallet a pile of bank-bills. Du Tillet looked furious. "You should never frown at money," said his impassible associate; "it brings ill-luck."

"Where did you get that money, madame?" said du Tillet, suddenly turning upon his wife with a look which made her color to the roots of her hair.

"I don't know what your question means," she said.

"I will fathom this mystery," he cried, springing furiously up. "You have upset my most cherished plans."

"You are upsetting your breakfast," said Gigonnet, arresting the table-clock, which was dragged by the skirt of du Tillet's dressing-gown.

Madame du Tillet rose to leave the room, for her husband's words alarmed her. She rang the bell, and a footman entered.

"The carriage," she said. "And call Virginie; I wish to dress."

"Where are you going?" exclaimed du Tillet.

"Well-bred husbands do not question their wives," she answered. "I believe that you lay claim to be a gentleman."

"I don't recognize you ever since you have seen more of your impertinent sister."

"You ordered me to be impertinent, and I am practising on you," she replied.

"Your servant, madame," said Gigonnet, taking leave, not anxious to witness this family scene.

Du Tillet looked fixedly at his wife, who returned the look without lowering her eyes.

"What does all this mean?" he said.

"It means that I am no longer a little girl whom you can frighten," she replied. "I am, and shall be, all my life, a good and loyal wife to you; you may be my master if you choose, my tyrant, never!"

Du Tillet left the room. After this effort Marie-Eugenie broke down.

"If it were not for my sister's danger," she said to herself, "I should never have dared to brave him thus; but, as the proverb says, 'There's some good in every evil.'"

CHAPTER IX

THE HUSBAND'S TRIUMPH

During the preceding night Madame du Tillet had gone over in her mind her sister's revelations. Sure, now, of Nathan's safety, she was no longer influenced by the thought of an imminent danger in that direction. But she remembered the vehement energy with which the countess had declared that she would fly with Nathan if that would save him. She saw that the man might determine her sister in some paroxysm of gratitude and love to take a step which was nothing short of madness. There were recent examples in the highest society of just such flights which paid for doubtful pleasures by lasting remorse and the disrepute of a false position. Du Tillet's speech brought her fears to a point; she dreaded lest all should be discovered; she knew her sister's signature was in Nucingen's hands, and she resolved to entreat Marie to save herself by confessing all to Felix.

She drove to her sister's house, but Marie was not at home. Felix was there. A voice within her cried aloud to Eugenie to save her sister; the morrow might be too late. She took a vast responsibility upon herself, but she resolved to tell all to the count. Surely he would be indulgent when he knew that his honor was still safe. The countess was deluded rather than sinful. Eugenie feared to be treacherous and base in revealing secrets that society (agreeing on this point) holds to be inviolable; but - she saw her sister's future, she trembled lest she should some day be deserted, ruined by Nathan, poor, suffering, disgraced, wretched, and she hesitated no longer; she sent in her name and asked to see the count.

Felix, astonished at the visit, had a long conversation with his sister-in-law, in which he seemed so calm, so completely master of himself, that she feared he might have taken some terrible resolution.

"Do not be uneasy," he said, seeing her anxiety. "I will act in a manner which shall make your sister bless you. However much you may dislike to keep the fact that you have spoken to me from her knowledge, I must entreat you to do so. I need a few days to search into mysteries which you don't perceive; and, above all, I must act cautiously. Perhaps I can learn all in a day. I, alone, my dear sister, am the guilty person. All lovers play their game, and it is not every woman who is able, unassisted, to see life as it is."

Madame du Tillet returned home comforted. Felix de Vandenesse drew forty thousand francs from the Bank of France, and went direct to Madame de Nucingen He found her at home, thanked her for the confidence she had placed in his wife, and returned the money, explaining that the countess had obtained this mysterious loan for her charities, which were so profuse that he was trying to put a limit to them.

"Give me no explanations, monsieur, since Madame de Vandenesse has told you all," said the Baronne de Nucingen.

"She knows the truth," thought Vandenesse.

Madame de Nucingen returned to him Marie's letter of
guarantee, and sent to the bank for the four notes.
Vandenesse, during the short time that these arrange-
ments kept him waiting, watched the baroness with the
eye of a statesman, and he thought the moment
propitious for further negotiation.

"We live in an age, madame, when nothing is sure," he
said. "Even thrones rise and fall in France with fearful
rapidity. Fifteen years have wreaked their will on a
great empire, a monarchy, and a revolution. No one
can now dare to count upon the future. You know my
attachment to the cause of legitimacy. Suppose some
catastrophe; would you not be glad to have a friend in
the conquering party?"

"Undoubtedly," she said, smiling.

"Very good; then, will you have in me, secretly, an
obliged friend who could be of use to Monsieur de
Nucingen in such a case, by supporting his claim to the
peerage he is seeking?"

"What do you want of me?" she asked.

"Very little," he replied. "All that you know about
Nathan's affairs."

The baroness repeated to him her conversation with
Rastignac, and said, as she gave him the four notes,
which the cashier had meantime brought to her:

"Don't forget your promise."

So little did Vandenesse forget this illusive promise that he used it again on Baron Eugene de Rastignac to obtain from him certain other information. Leaving Rastignac's apartments, he dictated to a street amanuensis the following note to Florine.

"If Mademoiselle Florine wishes to know of a part she may play she is requested to come to the masked opera at the Opera next Sunday night, accompanied by Monsieur Nathan."

To this ball he determined to take his wife and let her own eyes enlighten her as to the relations between Nathan and Florine. He knew the jealous pride of the countess; he wanted to make her renounce her love of her own will, without causing her to blush before him, and then to return to her her own letters, sold by Florine, from whom he expected to be able to buy them. This judicious plan, rapidly conceived and partly executed, might fail through some trick of chance which meddles with all things here below.

After dinner that evening, Felix brought the conversation round to the masked balls of the Opera, remarking that Marie had never been to one, and proposing that she should accompany him the following evening.

"I'll find you some one to 'intriguer,'" he said.

"Ah! I wish you would," she replied.

"To do the thing well, a woman ought to fasten upon some good prey, a celebrity, a man of enough wit to give and take. There's Nathan; will you have him? I know, through a friend of Florine, certain secrets of his which would drive him crazy."

"Florine?" said the countess. "Do you mean the actress?"

Marie had already heard that name from the lips of the watchman Quillet; it now shot like a flash of lightning through her soul.

"Yes, his mistress," replied the count. "What is there so surprising in that?"

"I thought Monsieur Nathan too busy to have a mistress. Do authors have time to make love?"

"I don't say they love, my dear, but they are forced to *lodge* somewhere, like other men, and when they haven't a home of their own they *lodge* with their mistresses; which may seem to you rather loose, but it is far more agreeable than lodging in a prison."

Fire was less red than Marie's cheeks.

"Will you have him for a victim? I can help you to terrify him," continued the count, not looking at his wife's face. "I'll put you in the way of proving to him that he is being tricked like a child by your brother-in-law du Tillet. That wretch is trying to put Nathan in prison so as to make him ineligible to stand against him in the electoral college. I know, through a friend of Florine, the exact sum derived from the sale of her furniture, which she gave to Nathan to found his newspaper; I know, too, what she sent him out of her summer's harvest in the departments and in Belgium, - money which has really gone to the profit of du Tillet, Nucingen, and Massol. All three of them, unknown to

Nathan, have privately sold the paper to the new ministry, so sure are they of ejecting him."

"Monsieur Nathan is incapable of accepting money from an actress."

"You don't know that class of people, my dear," said the count. "He would not deny the fact if you asked him."

"I will certainly go to the ball," said the countess.

"You will be very much amused," replied Vandenesse. "With such weapons in hand you can cut Nathan's complacency to the quick, and you will also do him a great service. You will put him in a fury; he'll try to be calm, though inwardly fuming; but, all the same, you will enlighten a man of talent as to the peril in which he really stands; and you will also have the satisfaction of laming the horses of the 'juste-milieu' in their stalls - But you are not listening to me, my dear."

"On the contrary, I am listening intently," she said. "I will tell you later why I feel desirous to know the truth of all this."

"You shall know it," said Vandenesse. "If you stay masked I will take you to supper with Nathan and Florine; it would be rather amusing for a woman of your rank to fool an actress after bewildering the wits of a clever man about these important facts; you can harness them both to the same hoax. I'll make some inquiries about Nathan's infidelities, and if I discover any of his recent adventures you shall enjoy the sight of a courtesan's fury; it is magnificent. Florine will boil and foam like an Alpine torrent; she adores Nathan; he is everything to her; she clings to him like flesh to the bones or a lioness to her cubs. I remember seeing, in my youth, a celebrated actress (who wrote like a scullion) when she came to a friend of mine to demand her letters. I have never seen such a sight again, such calm fury, such insolent majesty, such savage self-control - Are you ill, Marie?"

"No; they have made too much fire." The countess turned away and threw herself on a sofa. Suddenly, with an unforeseen movement, impelled by the horrible anguish of her jealousy, she rose on her trembling legs, crossed her arms, and came slowly to her husband.

"What do you know?" she asked. "You are not a man to torture me; you would crush me without making me suffer if I were guilty."

"What do you expect me to know, Marie?"

"Well! about Nathan."

"You think you love him," he replied; "but you love a phantom made of words."

"Then you know -"

"All," he said.

The word fell on Marie's head like the blow of a club.

"If you wish it, I will know nothing," he continued. "You are standing on the brink of a precipice, my child, and I must draw you from it. I have already done something. See!"

He drew from his pocket her letter of guarantee and the four notes endorsed by Schmucke, and let the countess recognize them; then he threw them into the fire.

"What would have happened to you, my poor Marie, three months hence?" he said. "The sheriffs would have taken you to a public court-room. Don't bow your head, don't feel humiliated; you have been the dupe of noble feelings; you have coquetted with poesy, not with a man. All women - all, do you hear me, Marie? - would have been seduced in your position. How absurd we should be, we men, we who have committed a thousand follies through a score of years, if we were not willing to grant you one imprudence in a lifetime! God keep me from triumphing over you or from offering you a pity you repelled so vehemently the other day. Perhaps that unfortunate man was sincere when he wrote to you, sincere in attempting to kill himself, sincere in returning that same night to Florine. Men are worth less than women. It is not for my own sake that I speak at this moment, but for yours. I am indulgent, but the world is not; it shuns a woman who makes a scandal. Is that just? I know not; but this I know, the world is cruel. Society refuses to calm the woes itself has caused; it gives its honors to those who best deceive it; it has no recompense for rash devotion. I see and know all that. I can't reform society, but this I can do, I can protect you, Marie, against yourself. This matter concerns a man who has brought you trouble only, and not one of those high and sacred loves which do, at times, command our abnegation, and even bear their own excuse. Perhaps I have been wrong in not varying your happiness, in not providing you with gayer pleasures, travel, amusements, distractions for the mind. Besides, I can explain to myself the impulse that has driven you to a celebrated man, by the jealous envy you have roused in certain women. Lady Dudley, Madame d'Espard, and my sister-in-law Emilie count for something in all this. Those women, against whom I ought to have put you more thoroughly on your guard, have cultivated your curiosity more to trouble me and cause me unhappiness, than to fling you into a whirlpool which, as I believe, you would never have entered."

As she listened to these words, so full of kindness, the countess was torn by many conflicting feelings; but the storm within her breast was ruled by one of them, - a keen admiration for her husband. Proud and noble souls are prompt to recognize the delicacy with which they are treated. Tact is to sentiments what grace is to the body. Marie appreciated the grandeur of the man who bowed before a woman in fault, that he might not see her blush. She ran from the room like one beside herself, but instantly returned, fearing lest her hasty action might cause him uneasiness.

"Wait," she said, and disappeared again.

Felix had ably prepared her excuse, and he was instantly rewarded for his generosity. His wife returned with Nathan's letters in her hand, and gave them to him.

"Judge me," she said, kneeling down beside him.

"Are we able to judge where we love?" he answered, throwing the letters into the fire; for he felt that later his wife might not forgive him for having read them. Marie, with her head upon his knee, burst into tears.

"My child," he said, raising her head, "where are

your letters?"

At this question the poor woman no longer felt the intolerable burning of her cheeks; she turned cold.

"That you may not suspect me of calumniating a man whom you think worthy of you, I will make Florine herself return you those letters."

"Oh! Surely he would give them back to me himself."

"Suppose that he refused to do so?"

The countess dropped her head.

"The world disgusts me," she said. "I don't want to enter it again. I want to live alone with you, if you forgive me."

"But you might get bored again. Besides, what would the world say if you left it so abruptly? In the spring we will travel; we will go to Italy, and all over Europe; you shall see life. But to-morrow night we must go to the Opera-ball; there is no other way to get those letters without compromising you; besides, by giving them up, Florine will prove to you her power."

"And must I see that?" said the countess, frightened.

"To-morrow night."

The next evening, about midnight, Nathan was walking about the foyer of the Opera with a mask on his arm, to whom he was attending in a sufficiently conjugal manner. Presently two masked women came up to him.

"You poor fool! Marie is here and is watching you," said one of them, who was Vandenesse, disguised as a woman.

"If you choose to listen to me I will tell you secrets that Nathan is hiding from you," said the other woman, who was the countess, to Florine.

Nathan had abruptly dropped Florine's arm to follow the count, who adroitly slipped into the crowd and was out of sight in a moment. Florine followed the countess, who sat down on a seat close at hand, to which the count, doubling on Nathan, returned almost immediately to guard his wife.

"Explain yourself, my dear," said Florine, "and don't think I shall stand this long. No one can tear Raoul from me, I'll tell you that; I hold him by habit, and that's even stronger than love."

"In the first place, are you Florine?" said the count, speaking in his natural voice.

"A pretty question! if you don't know that, my joking friend, why should I believe you?"

"Go and ask Nathan, who has left you to look for his other mistress, where he passed the night, three days ago. He tried to kill himself without a word to you, my dear, - and all for want of money. That shows how much you know about the affairs of a man whom you say you love, and who leaves you without a penny, and kills himself, - or, rather, doesn't kill himself, for his misses it. Suicides that don't kill are about as absurd as a duel without a scratch."

"That's a lie," said Florine. "He dined with me that very day. The poor fellow had the sheriff after him; he was hiding, as well he might."

"Go and ask at the hotel du Mail, rue du Mail, if he was not taken there that morning, half dead of the fumes of charcoal, by a handsome young woman with whom he has been in love over a year. Her letters are at this moment under your very nose in your own house. If you want to teach Nathan a good lesson, let us all three go there; and I'll show you, papers in hand, how you can save him from the sheriff and Clichy if you choose to be the good girl that you are."

"Try that on others than Florine, my little man. I am certain that Nathan has never been in love with any one but me."

"On the contrary, he has been in love with a woman in society for over a year -"

"A woman in society, he!" cried Florine. "I don't trouble myself about such nonsense as that."

"Well, do you want me to make him come and tell you that he will not take you home from here to-night."

"If you can make him tell me that," said Florine, "I'll take *you* home, and we'll look for those letters, which I shall believe in when I see them, and not till then. He must have written them while I slept."

"Stay here," said Felix, "and watch."

So saying, he took the arm of his wife and moved to a little distance. Presently, Nathan, who had been hunting up and down the foyer like a dog looking for its master, returned to the spot where the mask had addressed him. Seeing on his face an expression he could not conceal, Florine placed herself like a post in front of him, and said, imperiously: -

"I don't wish you to leave me again; I have my reasons for this."

The countess then, at the instigation of her husband, went up to Raoul and said in his ear, -

"Marie. Who is this woman? Leave her at once, and meet me at the foot of the grand staircase."

In this difficult extremity Raoul dropped Florine's arm, and though she caught his own and held it forcibly, she was obliged, after a moment, to let him go. Nathan disappeared into the crowd.

"What did I tell you?" said Felix in Florine's astonished ears, offering her his arm.

"Come," she said; "whoever you are, come. Have you a carriage here?"

For all answer, Vandenesse hurried Florine away, followed by his wife. A few moments later the three masks, driven rapidly by the Vandenesse coachman, reached Florine's house. As soon as she had entered her own apartments the actress unmasked. Madame de Vandenesse could not restrain a quiver of surprise at Florine's beauty as she stood there choking with anger, and superb in her wrath and jealousy.

"There is, somewhere in these rooms," said Vandenesse,

"a portfolio, the key of which you have never had; the letters are probably in it."

"Well, well, for once in my life I am bewildered; you know something that I have been uneasy about for some days," cried Florine, rushing into the study in search of the portfolio.

Vandenesse saw that his wife was turning pale beneath her mask. Florine's apartment revealed more about the intimacy of the actress and Nathan than any ideal mistress would wish to know. The eye of a woman can take in the truth of such things in a second, and the countess saw vestiges of Nathan which proved to her the certainty of what Vandenesse had said. Florine returned with the portfolio.

"How am I to open it?" she said.

The actress rang the bell and sent into the kitchen for the cook's knife. When it came she brandished it in the air, crying out in ironical tones: -

"With this they cut the necks of 'poulets.'"

The words, which made the countess shiver, explained to her, even better than her husband had done the night before, the depths of the abyss into which she had so nearly fallen.

"What a fool I am!" said Florine; "his razor will do better."

She fetched one of Nathan's razors from his dressing-table, and slit the leather cover of the portfolio, through which Marie's letters dropped. Florine snatched one up

Honore de Balzac

hap-hazard, and looked it over.

"Yes, she must be a well-bred woman. It looks to me as if there were no mistakes in spelling here."

The count gathered up the letters hastily and gave them to his wife, who took them to a table as if to see that they were all there.

"Now," said Vandenesse to Florine, "will you let me have those letters for these?" showing her five bank-bills of ten thousand francs each. "They'll replace the sums you have paid for him."

"Ah!" cried Florine, "didn't I kill myself body and soul in the provinces to get him money, - I, who'd have cut my hand off to serve him? But that's men! damn your soul for them and they'll march over you rough-shod! He shall pay me for this!"

Madame de Vandenesse was disappearing with the letters.

"Hi! stop, stop, my fine mask!" cried Florine; "leave me one to confound him with."

"Not possible," said Vandenesse.

"Why not?"

"That mask is your ex-rival; but you needn't fear her now."

"Well, she might have had the grace to say thank you," cried Florine.

"But you have the fifty thousand francs instead," said Vandenesse, bowing to her.

It is extremely rare for young men, when driven to suicide, to attempt it a second time if the first fails. When it doesn't cure life, it cures all desire for voluntary death. Raoul felt no disposition to try it again when he found himself in a more painful position than that from which he had just been rescued. He tried to see the countess and explain to her the nature of his love, which now shone more vividly in his soul than ever. But the first time they met in society, Madame de Vandenesse gave him that fixed and contemptuous look which at once and forever puts an impassable gulf between a man and a woman. In spite of his natural assurance, Nathan never dared, during the rest of the winter, either to speak to the countess or even approach her.

But he opened his heart to Blondet; to him he talked of his Laura and his Beatrice, apropos of Madame de Vandenesse. He even made a paraphrase of the following beautiful passage from the pen of Theophile Gautier, one of the most remarkable poets of our day: -

"'Ideala, flower of heaven's own blue, with heart of gold, whose fibrous roots, softer, a thousandfold, than fairy tresses, strike to our souls and drink their purest essence; flower most sweet and bitter! thou canst not be torn away without the heart's blood flowing, without thy bruised stems sweating with scarlet tears. Ah! Cursed flower, why didst thou grow within my soul?'"

"My dear fellow," said Blondet, "you are raving. I'll grant it was a pretty flower, but it wasn't a bit ideal, and instead of singing like a blind man before an empty niche, you had much better wash your hands and make submission to the powers. You are too much of an artist ever to be a good politician; you have been fooled by men of not one-half your value. Think about being fooled again - but elsewhere."

"Marie cannot prevent my loving her," said Nathan; "she shall be my Beatrice."

"Beatrice, my good Raoul, was a little girl twelve years of age when Dante last saw her; otherwise, she would not have been Beatrice. To make a divinity, it won't do to see her one day wrapped in a mantle, and the next with a low dress, and the third on the boulevard, cheapening toys for her last baby. When a man has Florine, who is in turn duchess, bourgeoise, Negress, marquise, colonel, Swiss peasant, virgin of the sun in Peru (only way she can play the part), I don't see why he should go rambling after fashionable women."

Du Tillet, to use a Bourse term, *executed* Nathan, who, for lack of money, gave up his place on the newspaper; and the celebrated man received but five votes in the electoral college where the banker was elected.

When, after a long and happy journey in Italy, the Comtesse de Vandenesse returned to Paris late in the following winter, all her husband's predictions about Nathan were justified. He had taken Blondet's advice and negotiated with the government, which employed his pen. His personal affairs were in such disorder that one day, on the Champs-Elysees, Marie saw her former adorer on foot, in shabby clothes, giving his arm to Florine. When a man becomes indifferent to the heart of a woman who has once loved him, he often seems to her very ugly, even horrible, especially when he resembles Nathan. Madame de Vandenesse had a sense of personal humiliation in the thought that she had once cared for him. If she had not already been cured of all extra-conjugal passion, the contrast then presented by the count to this man, grown less and less worthy of public favor, would have sufficed her.

To-day the ambitious Nathan, rich in ink and poor in will, has ended by capitulating entirely, and has settled down into a sinecure, like any other commonplace man. After lending his pen to all disorganizing efforts, he now lives in peace under the protecting shade of a ministerial organ. The cross of the Legion of honor, formerly the fruitful text of his satire, adorns his button-hole. "Peace at any price," ridicule of which was the stock-in-trade of his revolutionary editorship, is now the topic of his laudatory articles. Heredity, attacked by him in Saint-Simonian phrases, he now defends with solid arguments. This illogical conduct has its origin and its explanation in the change of front performed by many men besides Raoul during our recent political evolutions.

Choose from Thousands of 1stWorldLibrary Classics By

A. M. Barnard	C. M. Ingleby	Elizabeth Gaskell
Ada Leverson	Carolyn Wells	Elizabeth McCracken
Adolphus William Ward	Catherine Parr Traill	Elizabeth Von Arnim
Aesop	Charles A. Eastman	Ellem Key
Agatha Christie	Charles Amory Beach	Emerson Hough
Alexander Aaronsohn	Charles Dickens	Emilie F. Carlen
Alexander Kielland	Charles Dudley Warner	Emily Dickinson
Alexandre Dumas	Charles Farrar Browne	Enid Bagnold
Alfred Gatty	Charles Ives	Enilor Macartney Lane
Alfred Ollivant	Charles Kingsley	Erasmus W. Jones
Alice Duer Miller	Charles Klein	Ernie Howard Pie
Alice Turner Curtis	Charles Hanson Towne	Ethel May Dell
Alice Dunbar	Charles Lathrop Pack	Ethel Turner
Allen Chapman	Charles Romyn Dake	Ethel Watts Mumford
Ambrose Bierce	Charles Whibley	Eugenie Foa
Amelia E. Barr	Charles Willing Beale	Eugene Wood
Amory H. Bradford	Charlotte M. Braeme	Eustace Hale Ball
Andrew Lang	Charlotte M. Yonge	Evelyn Everett-green
Andrew McFarland Davis	Charlotte Perkins Stetson	Everard Cotes
Andy Adams	Clair W. Hayes	F. H. Cheley
Anna Alice Chapin	Clarence Day Jr.	F. J. Cross
Anna Sewell	Clarence E. Mulford	F. Marion Crawford
Annie Besant	Clemence Housman	Federick Austin Ogg
Annie Hamilton Donnell	Confucius	Ferdinand Ossendowski
Annie Payson Call	Coningsby Dawson	Francis Bacon
Annie Roe Carr	Cornelis DeWitt Wilcox	Francis Darwin
Annonanymous	Cyril Burleigh	Frances Hodgson Burnett
Anton Chekhov	D. H. Lawrence	Frances Parkinson Keyes
Arnold Bennett	Daniel Defoe	Frank Gee Patchin
Arthur Conan Doyle	David Garnett	Frank Harris
Arthur M. Winfield	Dinah Craik	Frank Jewett Mather
Arthur Ransome	Don Carlos Janes	Frank L. Packard
Arthur Schnitzler	Donald Keyhoe	Frank V. Webster
Atticus	Dorothy Kilner	Frederic Stewart Isham
B.H. Baden-Powell	Dougan Clark	Frederick Trevor Hill
B. M. Bower	Douglas Fairbanks	Frederick Winslow Taylor
B. C. Chatterjee	E. Nesbit	Friedrich Kerst
Baroness Emmuska Orczy	E.P.Roe	Friedrich Nietzsche
Baroness Orczy	E. Phillips Oppenheim	Fyodor Dostoyevsky
Basil King	Earl Barnes	G.A. Henty
Bayard Taylor	Edgar Rice Burroughs	G.K. Chesterton
Ben Macomber	Edith Van Dyne	Gabrielle E. Jackson
Bertha Muzzy Bower	Edith Wharton	Garrett P. Serviss
Bjornstjerne Bjornson	Edward Everett Hale	Gaston Leroux
Booth Tarkington	Edward J. O'Biren	George A. Warren
Boyd Cable	Edward S. Ellis	George Ade
Bram Stoker	Edwin L. Arnold	Geroge Bernard Shaw
C. Collodi	Eleanor Atkins	George Durston
C. E. Orr	Eliot Gregory	George Ebers

George Eliot	Herbert Carter	John Habberton
George Gissing	Herbert N. Casson	John Joy Bell
George MacDonald	Herman Hesse	John Kendrick Bangs
George Meredith	Hildegard G. Frey	John Milton
George Orwell	Homer	John Philip Sousa
George Sylvester Viereck	Honore De Balzac	Jonas Lauritz Idemil Lie
George Tucker	Horace B. Day	Jonathan Swift
George W. Cable	Horace Walpole	Joseph A. Altsheler
George Wharton James	Horatio Alger Jr.	Joseph Carey
Gertrude Atherton	Howard Pyle	Joseph Conrad
Gordon Casserly	Howard R. Garis	Joseph E. Badger Jr
Grace E. King	Hugh Lofting	Joseph Hergesheimer
Grace Gallatin	Hugh Walpole	Joseph Jacobs
Grace Greenwood	Humphry Ward	Jules Vernes
Grant Allen	Ian Maclaren	Julian Hawthrone
Guillermo A. Sherwell	Inez Haynes Gillmore	Julie A Lippmann
Gulielma Zollinger	Irving Bacheller	Justin Huntly McCarthy
Gustav Flaubert	Isabel Hornibrook	Kakuzo Okakura
H. A. Cody	Israel Abrahams	Kenneth Grahame
H. B. Irving	Ivan Turgenev	Kenneth McGaffey
H.C. Bailey	J.G.Austin	Kate Langley Bosher
H. G. Wells	J. Henri Fabre	Kate Langley Bosher
H. H. Munro	J. M. Barrie	Katherine Cecil Thurston
H. Irving Hancock	J. Macdonald Oxley	Katherine Stokes
H. Rider Haggard	J. S. Fletcher	L. A. Abbot
H. W. C. Davis	J. S. Knowles	L. T. Meade
Haldeman Julius	J. Storer Clouston	L. Frank Baum
Hall Caine	Jack London	Latta Griswold
Hamilton Wright Mabie	Jacob Abbott	Laura Dent Crane
Hans Christian Andersen	James Allen	Laura Lee Hope
Harold Avery	James Andrews	Laurence Housman
Harold McGrath	James Baldwin	Lawrence Beasley
Harriet Beecher Stowe	James Branch Cabell	Leo Tolstoy
Harry Castlemon	James DeMille	Leonid Andreyev
Harry Coghill	James Joyce	Lewis Carroll
Harry Houidini	James Lane Allen	Lewis Sperry Chafer
Hayden Carruth	James Lane Allen	Lilian Bell
Helent Hunt Jackson	James Oliver Curwood	Lloyd Osbourne
Helen Nicolay	James Oppenheim	Louis Hughes
Hendrik Conscience	James Otis	Louis Tracy
Hendy David Thoreau	James R. Driscoll	Louisa May Alcott
Henri Barbusse	Jane Austen	Lucy Fitch Perkins
Henrik Ibsen	Jane L. Stewart	Lucy Maud Montgomery
Henry Adams	Janet Aldridge	Luther Benson
Henry Ford	Jens Peter Jacobsen	Lydia Miller Middleton
Henry Frost	Jerome K. Jerome	Lyndon Orr
Henry James	John Burroughs	M. Corvus
Henry Jones Ford	John Cournos	M. H. Adams
Henry Seton Merriman	John F. Kennedy	Margaret E. Sangster
Henry W Longfellow	John Gay	Margret Howth
Herbert A. Giles	John Glasworthy	Margaret Vandercook

Margret Penrose
Maria Edgeworth
Maria Thompson Daviess
Mariano Azuela
Marion Polk Angellotti
Mark Overton
Mark Twain
Mary Austin
Mary Catherine Crowley
Mary Cole
Mary Hastings Bradley
Mary Roberts Rinehart
Mary Rowlandson
M. Wollstonecraft Shelley
Maud Lindsay
Max Beerbohm
Myra Kelly
Nathaniel Hawthrone
Nicolo Machiavelli
O. F. Walton
Oscar Wilde
Owen Johnson
P.G. Wodehouse
Paul and Mabel Thorne
Paul G. Tomlinson
Paul Severing
Percy Brebner
Peter B. Kyne
Plato
R. Derby Holmes
R. L. Stevenson
R. S. Ball
Rabindranath Tagore
Rahul Alvares
Ralph Bonehill
Ralph Henry Barbour
Ralph Victor
Ralph Waldo Emmerson
Rene Descartes
Rex Beach

Rex E. Beach
Richard Harding Davis
Richard Jefferies
Richard Le Gallienne
Robert Barr
Robert Frost
Robert Gordon Anderson
Robert L. Drake
Robert Lansing
Robert Lynd
Robert Michael Ballantyne
Robert W. Chambers
Rosa Nouchette Carey
Rudyard Kipling
Samuel B. Allison
Samuel Hopkins Adams
Sarah Bernhardt
Sarah C. Hallowell
Selma Lagerlof
Sherwood Anderson
Sigmund Freud
Standish O'Grady
Stanley Weyman
Stella Benson
Stella M. Francis
Stephen Crane
Stewart Edward White
Stijn Streuvels
Swami Abhedananda
Swami Parmananda
T. S. Ackland
T. S. Arthur
The Princess Der Ling
Thomas A. Janvier
Thomas A Kempis
Thomas Anderton
Thomas Bailey Aldrich
Thomas Bulfinch
Thomas De Quincey
Thomas Dixon

Thomas H. Huxley
Thomas Hardy
Thomas More
Thornton W. Burgess
U. S. Grant
Valentine Williams
Various Authors
Vaughan Kester
Victor Appleton
Victoria Cross
Virginia Woolf
Wadsworth Camp
Walter Camp
Walter Scott
Washington Irving
Wilbur Lawton
Wilkie Collins
Willa Cather
Willard F. Baker
William Dean Howells
William le Queux
W. Makepeace Thackeray
William W. Walter
William Shakespeare
Winston Churchill
Yei Theodora Ozaki
Yogi Ramacharaka
Young E. Allison
Zane Grey

www.ingramcontent.com/pod-product-compliance
Lightning Source LLC
Chambersburg PA
CBHW020504100426
42813CB00030B/3105/J